LIBRARY OF CONGRESS

Hispanic and Portuguese Collections

AN ILLUSTRATED GUIDE

LIBRARY OF CONGRESS WASHINGTON 1996

This publication was made possible by generous support from the James Madison Council, a national, private-sector advisory council dedicated to helping the Library of Congress share its unique resources with the nation and the world.

Hispanic and Portuguese Collections is composed in Centaur, a typeface designed by American typography and book designer Bruce Rogers (1870–1957). The full type font was first used at the Montague Press in 1915 for an edition of Maurice de Guérin's *The Centaur*.

This guide was designed by Robert Wiser, Archetype Press, Inc., Washington, D.C.

COVER: *Detail from the first page of the manuscript Columbus's Book of Privileges. Vellum. Sevilla, ca. 1502.* This is Columbus's archival collection of documents by which Queen Isabel and King Fernando granted titles, revenues, powers, and privileges to him and his descendants. The document shown is part of Pope Alexander VI's 1493 papal bull granting Spain exclusive rights in what came to be called America. See page 7 for the complete page and citation.

LIBRARY OF CONGRESS CATALOGING-IN-PUBLICATION DATA

Library of Congress.
   Library of Congress Hispanic and Portuguese collections : an illustrated guide.
      p.   cm.
   ISBN 0–8444–0881–6
   ——— ——— Copy 3 Z663 .L456   1996
      1. Spain — Library resources. 2. Portugal — Library resources. 3. Latin America — Library resources. 4. Spain — Colonies — Library resources. 5. Portugal — Colonies — Library resources. 6. Library of Congress. 7. Library resources — Washington (D.C.) I. Title.
      Z2681.L48   1996
      [DP17]   96–18095
      027'.573—dc20   CIP

For sale by the U.S. Government Printing Office
Superintendent of Documents
Mail Stop: SSOP, Washington, D.C. 20402–9328

Contents

Introduction

THE LIBRARY OF CONGRESS is an extraordinary resource for substantive primary research in virtually any field or area of Hispanic and Portuguese studies (commonly referred to as Luso-Hispanic studies after the Latin names for both entities of the Iberian Peninsula, i.e., Portugal was Lusitania and Spain was Hispania), encompassing Latin America, the Caribbean, Hispanics and Portuguese in the United States, the Iberian Peninsula, and other places where Iberian culture dominated and has survived. I will interchangeably refer to our collections as Hispanic and Portuguese collections or as Luso-Hispanic collections. Within its total Hispanic and Portuguese collections of ten million items are an estimated one million related books and periodicals on Latin America alone and an equal number for the Iberian Peninsula and the rest of the Luso-Hispanic world. For books, maps, and for retrospective holdings of government serials (national and provincial), newspapers, and other periodicals, these are the most extensive collections in the world. So voluminous and diverse are the Library's Luso-Hispanic holdings that it is practically impossible to itemize or categorize adequately significant topical or geographic strengths. Suffice it to say that visiting Iberian and Latin American scholars consistently report the discovery of materials in the Library of Congress that are not available in their home countries.

The Library of Congress's collections reflect admirably on the early wishes of the Congress of the United States to remain informed about the cultures, places, things, and societies outside of the territory of the United States that affect our society, either through direct contact or from afar. At its inception in 1800 the Library of Congress reflected a worldview in its collecting patterns, even before the acquisition of Thomas Jefferson's personal library in 1815, following the destruction of the Library by invading British forces. Over these past two hundred years the Library of Congress's Hispanic and Portuguese collections have become unparalleled in their content, breadth, and scope.

These Hispanic and Portuguese collections describe broadly and deeply Native American cultures; the cultures of the independent states of Latin America and the Caribbean; the colonial histories of Spain, Portugal, France, and England in what is now the Caribbean, the United States, and Latin America; a myriad body of material on the literature, art, law, and politics of the Iberian Peninsula; and a treasure trove of rare books, manuscripts, and maps about Spanish and Portuguese exploration, discovery, and expansion globally, from Lucena's 1488 work on Portuguese exploration and Christopher Columbus's own 1502 manuscript book of privileges, to contemporary manuscript accounts of Pedro Alvares Cabral's voyage to Brazil and India in 1500.

PRECEDING PAGES. *Vue de la Place vieille/Vista de la Plaza Vieja [Havana, Cuba]. In Hippolite J. B. Garnerey. Vues de la Habana. Paris 1830.* The industrious, bustling, multicultural center of trade in Havana is depicted in this view. Additional information about the city, with various cultural information provided, appears in the work, which provides a period snapshot of nineteenth-century urban Cuba. (*Geography and Map Division*)

First page. In [Christopher Columbus] [Códice Diplomático Columbo-Americano]. Vellum. [Sevilla, ca. 1502]. Undoubtedly the Library of Congress's most prized early Americana. The manuscript cited is commonly referred to as *Columbus's Book of Privileges.* On January 5, 1502, Columbus gathered at his home in Seville two local judges and three notaries to authorize the preparation of authentic copies of his archival collection of documents by which Queen Isabel and King Fernando had granted titles, revenues, powers, and privileges to him and his descendants. Columbus was then preparing to embark on his fourth and final voyage to America. Through this compilation he hoped to protect his future interest in wealth and honors by placing authenticated copies of these documents in trusted hands. We know that four copies of his compilation existed in 1502, three written on vellum and one on paper. The Library of Congress copy, acquired from William Everett in 1901, is the only example in the Western Hemisphere and is the one item in the Library's collection known to have been in Columbus's hands. A unique copy of the September 26, 1493 Papal Bull *Dudum siquidem* distinguishes the Library of Congress copy of the *Book of Privileges* from all others. The other two vellum copies are located in Paris and in Genoa. *(Manuscript Division)*

Warriors enlisted for military campaign. Amate paper. Huexotzinco Codex. 1531. A codex, a Mesoamerican written document containing historical, calendrical, or other forms of information, is pre-European in origin. The codices were made by a writer known as the tlacauilo who had stature in the community. With the arrival of the Spaniards, the use of the codex as a written form gradually diminished during the sixteenth century as the romanized written Mexica (nahuatl) replaced it. In the *Huexotzinco Codex* one can see a number of interesting features of the Indian society, e.g., in the plate displayed, the use of the banner or flag represents the number twenty and therefore each flag refers to twenty warriors. Other sheets of the codex provide additional symbols for the numbers 400 and 8000. The *Huexotzinco Codex* is among the priceless documents found in the Harkness Collection, given to the Library of Congress in 1928 and 1929. *(Harkness Collection, Manuscript Division)*

Special thanks are extended to Georgette Dorn, Chief, and specialists Everette Larson, Barbara Tenenbaum, and Iêda Siqueira Wiarda whose suggestions and additions have improved this work. Additionally, I appreciate the assistance of the specialists in the Library's various special collections who willingly provided invaluable information about Luso-Hispanic materials in their rich collections and of Iris Newsom, editor, Publishing Office, whose deft hand and critical eye have immeasurably improved this work. Finally, to you the user of the guide, I hope that it provides to you a brief but enticing glimpse to the dimensions of the treasures and the resources that comprise the Library of Congress's Hispanic and Portuguese collections.

JOHN R. HÉBERT
SENIOR SPECIALIST IN HISPANIC BIBLIOGRAPHY
HISPANIC DIVISION

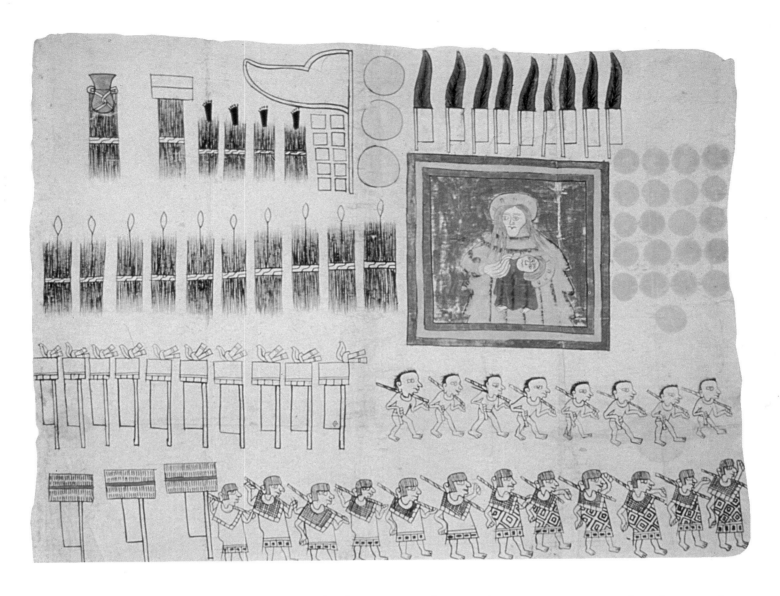

Products and services provided as tribute, including a banner with Madonna and Child. Amate paper. Huexotzinco Codex. Indian peoples of Mexico were accustomed to paying tribute to the pre-European Mexica (Aztec) Empire and that custom prevailed during the Spanish period. The people of Huexotzinco, along with Hernando Cortés, won a legal suit against the Spanish crown who had imposed excessive taxes. The *Huexotzinco Codex*, prepared in the time-honored fashion of pre-European Meso America, is the graphic portion of the lawsuit. The sheet depicted contains one of the earliest known images of the Madonna and Child in this type of document, a representation of an expensive banner made of precious feathers and gold. Produced only ten years after Conquest, it is a valuable document for a deeper understanding of the dramatic transitions that took place during Mexico's early colonial period. *(Harkness Collection, Manuscript Division)*

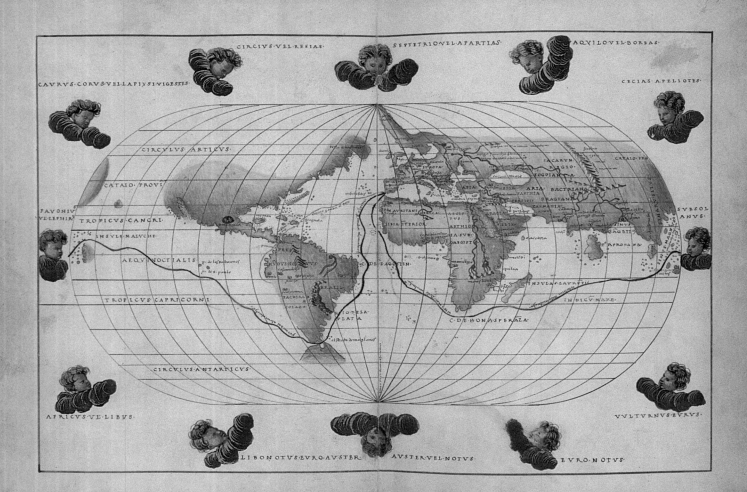

CIRCIVS·VEL·RESIAS·   SEPTETRIO·VEL·APARTIAS·   AQVILO·VEL·BORBAS·

CAVRVS·CORVS·VELLAPIVSI·VIGESTES·   CECIAS·APELIOTES·

FAVONIV VELEPHIR   SVBSOL ANVS·

CIRCVLVS·ARTICVS·

CATAIO·PROVI

TROPICVS·CANCRI·

INSVLA·MALVCHE

AEQVINOCTIALIS·

TROPICVS·CAPRICORNI·

INDICVMARE

CIRCVLVS·ANTARTICVS·

AFRICVS·VE·LIBVS·   VVLTVRNVS·EVRVS·

LIBONOTVS·EVRO·AVSTER   AVSTER·VEL·NOTVS·   EVRO·NOTVS·

General Overview

THE HISPANIC AND PORTUGUESE COLLECTIONS encompass research materials related to the societies (histories, cultures, languages) of the Iberian peninsula, Latin America and the Caribbean, and those areas where Spain and Portugal ruled—Angola and Mozambique, Damão, Goa, Diu, Philippines, Macao, and parts of the United States that were once Spanish territory.

Separate, considerable collections of manuscripts, pamphlets, journals, newspapers, or books can serve independently as sources of study of many subjects. However, it is in the integration of such materials and media for research that real advancement of knowledge is possible. That is the true strength of the Luso-Hispanic collections and even superlatives are insufficient to describe them.

While it is universally accepted that the basis of the collection was the genius of Thomas Jefferson, the Library of Congress's foundation predates the Jefferson Library purchase. And yet, Jefferson did possess extraordinarily significant publications both on the contemporary and the historical Luso-Hispanic world. He possessed a copy of Cruz Cano y Olmedilla's famous 1775 map of South America, which he had printed in facsimile in 1799 in London because the original was not available through Spanish sources. The practically two hundred-year-old collections are especially important for understanding the Americas, the Iberian Peninsula, and other regions of the world in which there exists long-term Hispanic and Portuguese influence. The first American imprints, from Mexico and from Peru, appear. Reproductions of codices of the pre-European American societies are found. The early cartographic renderings of America fromCanada to Tierra del Fuego and early geographic knowledge for Iberia and its advances in the Eastern Hemisphere emerge. The presence of Muslim, Jewish, and Christian cultures in Iberia, the development of glossaries and dictionaries, and advances in the history of science in Europe through Iberian sources are contained in this remarkable body of cultural output.

The collections are not restricted by chronology. In the holdings, original manuscripts or codices on America prepared after 1492 appear. Precious reproductions of pre-European written documents—codices—by indigenous peoples are collected extensively, and original pre-European musical instruments from Mayan and Andean sources are found in the Music Division. Similarly, the collection of original materials from Iberia, both printed and manuscript, date from the fourteenth and the fifteenth centuries. That historical record of the vast stages of human development in the Iberian Peninsula and in Latin America, prepared since the mid-fifteenth century, is extraordinarily rich.

The Library's collections, unlike those of an archive or a museum, include

OPPOSITE. *World Map with Route of Magellan. In Battista Agnese. [Portolan Atlas]. Venice, ca. 1544.* This chart of the world, with Magellan's route of circumnavigation included, depicted the extent of new found knowledge regarding the world that Mediterranean explorers obtained within fifty years of Columbus's 1492 contact in America. The former Europocentric world view had fallen victim to new ideas and places. Known as Ferdinand Magellan to the English-speaking world, Fernão de Magalhães was a Portuguese navigator sailing for Spain. (*Vellum Chart Collection, Geography and Map Division*)

OPPOSITE. *Americae sive quartae orbis partis nova et exactissima descriptio [Map of America]. Diego Gutiérrez. 1562.* The *Casa de Contratación* in Seville was the central authority for Spanish travel to America and custodian of charts and sailing directions for the Western Hemisphere. Diego Gutiérrez, hijo, was a chart and instrument maker and a pilot who worked in the *Casa de Contratación* from about 1554 until the 1570s. His 1562 map of America was engraved by Hieronymus Cock, a Flemish artist born in Antwerp in 1510. Gutiérrez's map, of which the Library of Congress holds only one of two extant, relied upon the collection of data acquired by Spain in America which provided the most up-to-date information on the people, settlements, and other geographical features of the Atlantic and Gulf coasts of North America, all of Central and South America, and portions of the western coasts of Africa. The map was a key Spanish document showing its American possessions following the Treaty of Cateau-Cambresis (1559). *(Geography and Map Division)*

recent research contributions, thereby providing a complementary body of research materials for serious study. This extraordinary body of material has been supplemented by benefactions that have further strengthened it, in many cases providing the original printed or manuscript document that has been the subject of later study, as for example, in materials related to Christopher Columbus, early printing on and in America, exploration in America, or the changing composition of Luso-Hispanic cultures. The Library's collections, especially in relation to America, are significant in providing the materials necessary for analyzing the varied understandings of what came to be called America and continuing broad research interests on a variety of topics related to America.

The Library of Congress contains treasures for the serious researcher as well as extensive holdings of documents that reflect upon the five hundred-year presence of Spanish and Portuguese societies in the Americas and the very rich cultures of indigenous Americans, Africans, Asians, and other European peoples who occupy the region. Equally, the history of Spain and Portugal, with their multiple cultures within the Iberian Peninsula as well as elsewhere in Europe, Africa, and Asia is strongly represented.

The collections include rich holdings in the area of recorded knowledge of the peoples of Hispanic and Portuguese origin in the United States, from the initial Spanish presence in what is now the United States to continuing incidents of arrival. Our collections, because of their early establishment, mirror the changes occurring in Luso-Hispanic America during the entire national period, with full records of governmental publications, gazettes, and newspapers of the nineteenth and twentieth centuries that allow considerable in-depth research.

Thomas Jefferson, whose private collection served as one of the cornerstones of the Library, felt a special concern for books on the Americas. He believed in the basic unity of the Western Hemisphere and understood the need for a special relationship among the American republics. As early as 1809 he wrote that "Mexico is one of the most interesting countries of our hemisphere, and merits our attention." And in 1820 he declared further that "I should rejoice to see the fleets of Brazil and the United States riding together as brethren of the same family and pursuing the same object."

The library sold by Jefferson, rich in books about the regions of the world and relating to most branches of knowledge, included almost two hundred volumes about Spanish and Portuguese America, the Caribbean, and the Iberian Peninsula, in Spanish, French, Italian, or Latin, all languages which the former president read with ease. Jefferson possessed an insatiable curiosity about America, and in his

attempt to learn as much as possible about the diversity of human societies, as well as the environment of the region, and the conquest of a large portion of it by Spain and Portugal, he had amassed a learned collection of books and maps. He believed that it was important for North Americans to learn Spanish because "our future connection with Spain and Spanish America will render that language a valuable acquisition," and he also stated that one ought to keep in mind that much of the history of the Americas was written in Spanish. Both the collections of the original congressional library, organized to meet the demands of the legislators for law and general literature, and Jefferson's library, which expanded considerably the subject and language scope of the collections, held primarily contemporary, scholarly editions.

After the war between the United States and Mexico (1846–1848) there existed a practical need to acquire information about the latter country. On August 4, 1848, the Joint Committee of Congress on the Library resolved that "the Librarian be authorized to purchase all the constitutions and laws of Mexico, and also to subscribe for a newspaper published in Vera Cruz and for one published in the City of Mexico." The acquisition of the Peter Force collection in the 1860s brought additional historical materials on the Americas to the Library, including nineteenth-century manuscript copies of Fray Diego Durán's 1585 *Historia Antigua de la Nueva España*, Fray Jerónimo de Alcalá's 1537–1541 *Relación de las ceremonias y ritos y población y gobierno de los indios de la provincia de Mechuacán*, and Mariano Fernández de Echevarría y Veitia's eighteenth-century *Historia del origen de las gentes que poblaron la América septentrional*.

The opening of the Library of Congress building in 1897, now the Thomas Jefferson Building, led to a reexamination of the purposes and possibilities of the institution. New departments for Manuscripts, Maps, and Music were created. As part of that reexamination, Librarian of Congress John Russell Young recognized the need for special development of materials related to the nations of the Western Hemisphere:

The interblending of Spanish-American history with that of the United States makes it advisable that we should continue to strengthen ourselves in that department . . . It would be wise to the development of the manuscript department to note particularly what pertains not only to the United States, but to America in general, Canada, Newfoundland, Nova Scotia, the West Indies, but more especially the countries to the south—Mexico, Central America and South America. . . .

Knowledge of the Library's growing specialization in the Hispanic and Portuguese field began to attract important gifts. The family of Ephraim George

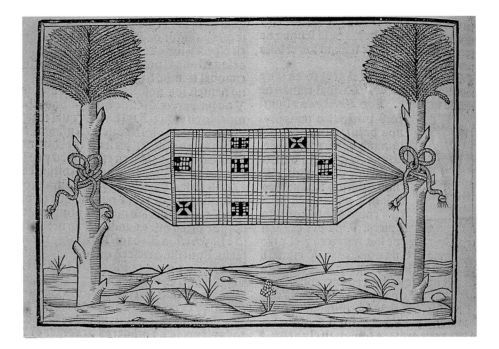

Hammock. *Gonzalo Fernández de Oviedo y Valdés. La Historia general y natural de las Indias . . . Seville, 1535.* Oviedo sailed in 1514 on his first of many journeys to America, where for over thirty years he compiled detailed ethnographic descriptions of such an innumerable list of products and goods, peoples and customs that he found it "almost impossible to write . . . given the abundance of ideas that come to mind." He introduced Europe to an enormous variety of previously unheard of American exotica, including the pineapple, the canoe, smoking tobacco, the manatee, and the hammock. Along with Pedro Mártir de Anglería and Bartolomé de Las Casas, Oviedo was one of the first European "chroniclers of the Indies". The Library of Congress acquired this rare autographed copy of *Historia* in 1867. *(Rare Book and Special Collections Division)*

Squier gave to the Library the papers of this pioneer American anthropologist and U.S. diplomat, including over two thousand letters from correspondents principally relating to the indigenous histories of the Americas, especially of Peru, Central America, and Mexico. The Henry Harrisse bequest of 1915 added the correspondence and profusely annotated copies of the many writings of this scholar of Columbus and the early colonial period of the Americas.

In 1926 the Library published a desiderata list of what Librarian of Congress Herbert Putnam termed "bibliographical monumenta, which should indisputably be represented in the National Library of the United States." That list, which includes such rarities as Columbus's 1493 printed account of his first voyage to America, has served as a major collection focus for rare Luso-Hispanic works. Over the years, through gifts and purchases, the Library of Congress has been able to acquire many imprints on the list.

In 1927, Archer M. Huntington, Hispanist, poet, and president of the Hispanic Society of America, established the Huntington Endowment Fund as the first of several important donations. The interest from this gift continues to be devoted annually to the purchase of books related to Spanish, Portuguese, and Latin American arts, crafts, literature, and history published during the past ten years.

Huntington gave the Library a second endowment the following year to facilitate the selection and servicing of those materials and helped create a

Come ce peuple couppe et porte le Brésil es navires. Engraving. André Thevet. Cosmographie universelle illustrée des diverses figures des choses les plus remarquables . . . ,1575. vol. 2. Paris. In 1555 André Thevet, a Franciscan priest, sailed with a small group of Frenchmen under the command of Villegagnon to found a colony, a southern New France, on the Brazilian coast. Thevet reported his observations of the agriculture, customs, and language of the indigenous people of that region. This illustration gives some idea of the labor involved in the cutting down and transporting of brazilwood to European ships on the coast. As Thevet relates, "when merchants get there, be they French, Spanish, or other Europeans . . . they trade with the savages [in order to get them] to cut down and carry the Brazilwood. The ships are sometimes a long distance from where they cut the wood . . . and all the profits that these poor people get for such effort, is a miserable little shirt, or some other item of dress of little value." *(Rare Book and Special Collections Division)*

consultantship in Spanish and Portuguese literature. The first appointee was Juan Riaño y Gayangos, a distinguished Spanish diplomat who had served from 1914 to 1926 as ambassador of his government to the United States.

In the first year of the appointment, the Library received two significant gifts from Edward S. Harkness, who donated a magnificent collection of Spanish manuscripts relating to the early colonial history of Mexico and Peru, and from John D. Rockefeller, Jr., who provided funds for the photocopying of foreign archival manuscripts relating to the history of America, the result being that many manuscripts concerning the sixteenth- to nineteenth-century history of the United States's southeastern and southwestern areas were copied in Mexico, Spain, France, England, Germany, and Austria.

Father David Rubio served as consultant from 1931 to 1943 and, for the period 1939–1943, was curator of the Hispanic and Portuguese collections. Rubio, with the use of the Huntington acquisition funds, helped the collections grow from 15,000 to more than 100,000 monographic volumes, and unprecedented efforts were made to develop further special groups of material. An example of that effort was the work of John Lomax, who enriched the Archive of American Folk Song in the American Folklife Reading Room by collecting Hispanic folk music, including a San Antonio, Texas, version of *Las Posadas* and the *Los Pastores* miracle play.

It was while Father Rubio was serving as consultant in Spanish and Portuguese literature that Archer Huntington gave the Library of Congress a monetary grant for the construction of the Hispanic Room and a trust fund for its maintenance. Father Rubio provided a graphic description of how the decision for those commitments was made:

After five years of work and several journeys to Spain and Portugal we now had some one hundred thousand volumes in the Hispanic Section, whereas there were no more than fifteen thousand when I had begun. From Latin America there had not been even a single volume of Rubén Darío. Dr. Putnam [the Librarian of Congress], very pleased with my labor, informed Mr. Huntington of the state and progress of his foundation and invited him to pay a visit. Putnam and I were in the central office awaiting him . . . After lunch . . . we walked around Deck A, where the Semitic Division was then located. On seeing it, Huntington asked: "Where is the Hispanic Division?" I replied: "We are waiting for some Mecenas [patron of the arts] to help us found it . . . " Mr. Huntington said goodby to us and some months later the director of the Library called me to his office and said: "We have here a new gift from Mr. Huntington to create a special room dedicated to Hispanic culture."

The establishment of the Hispanic Foundation in 1939 was a natural outcome of generations of collection development that had begun in 1800. The Hispanic Room, designed by the architect Paul Philipe Cret and completed in 1939, was intended to draw the researcher into the beauty of the Spanish and Portuguese Renaissance reflecting the taste of sixteenth- and seventeenth-century Iberia, through its vaulted ceiling, wood panelled alcoves, a dado of Puebla blue tile, and wrought iron balconies. The room was dedicated on October 12, 1939. In his address, Librarian of Congress Archibald MacLeish emphasized the oneness of the Americas and the need for Americans, both north and south, to appreciate their land for its own merits. To those living in the United States he presented the challenge of learning about the other American past, a past that defended human liberty at a time when witches were being hanged in Salem. In his eyes, Latin America shared with the United States the "unforgettable experience of the journey toward the West and the westward hope." He saw, in the Hispanic Room, a place where students of the Americas could follow the great Hispanic tradition that, with its ideas and its poetry, had populated "by far the

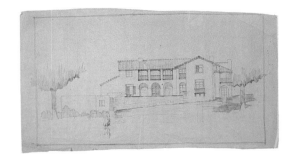

Home design, Spanish revival architecture. Watercolor over pen and ink, ca. 1920s. Santa Barbara, California. During the 1920s, in both the southwestern and the southeastern regions of the United States, there arose a renewed wave of interest in creating homes and other buildings in the style of Spain. In this depiction of a house type in California or in the rebuilding of St. Augustine, Florida, we see the earlier Spanish form that became popular. (Prints and Photographs Division)

"Teaching of the Indians" and "Mining of Gold." Cândido Portinari. [1941]. Portinari Murals. Portinari, through his canvases, murals, and tile walls, devoted his energies to the explanation of the mysteries and attractions of the forgotten peoples. Through his four murals in the Hispanic Division he relates central themes in the past 500 year experience of human contact in the Americas: exploration and discovery, conquering the environment, acculturation and cross-cultural fertilization, and exploitation of natural resources. *(Foyer, Hispanic Division)*

greater part of these two continents." He closed his remarks by appealing for a universal brotherhood of the human spirit.

There are men in the world today—and many rather than few—who say that the proper study of mankind is not man but a particular kind of man. There are those who teach that the only cultural study proper to a great people is its own culture. There are those also who say that the only real brotherhood is that blood brotherhood for which so many wars have been fought and by which so many deaths are still justified. The dedication of this room and of this collection of books is a demonstration of the fact that these opinions are not valid in the Americas: that in the Americas, peopled by so many sufferings, so many races, the highest brotherhood is still the brotherhood of the human spirit and the true study is the study of the best.

At the time of the Hispanic Room's dedication, it was hoped that the two vestibules could be decorated by a Latin American artist. Cândido Portinari, the outstanding Brazilian muralist, was selected to prepare four large paintings, which he completed between October 1941 and January 12, 1942. In designing the murals, Portinari imposed the restriction that the figures and the objects be so represented as to apply not to one age alone but to the whole succession of periods since the arrival of the Spaniards and Portuguese in America. Through four panels, *Discovery of the Land, Entry into the Forest, Teaching of the Indians,* and *Mining of Gold,* the muralist represented Indian, black, and white peoples in America.

It is evident that over the years the Library of Congress has been assembling remarkable Hispanic and Portuguese collections, located throughout the Library;

in its Hispanic Division and other area studies divisions, in the special collections, and within the general books collection. These collections have been assembled and continue to be enhanced by timely donations of rare and unique treasures and by consistent acquisition of contemporary items through purchase, exchange, and the efforts of the Library of Congress's overseas offices. An office was established in Rio de Janeiro in 1966 which has had a major impact on the quantity and the quality of our Brasiliana collection.

In the Library's Rare Book and Special Collections Division, there are copies of the earliest books printed in America—the 1544 Mexican imprints, Juan de Zumárraga's *Doctrina breve muy provechosa*, Juan de Gerson's *Tripartito del christianissimo y consolatorio doctor Juan Gerson de doctrina christiana*, and Denis la Chartreux's *Este es un copedio [sic] breve que tracta.* . . . Two of the earliest books printed in South America, in Lima, form part of the collection: Luís López's 1585 *Tercero Cathecismo y exposición de la doctrina Christiana* and Antonio Ricardo's 1586 *Vocabulario en la lengua general del Peru llamada Quichua.* Among Spanish incunabula are a 1491 edition of the *Siete Partidas* and Fernán de Mexía's book of noble families (1492). The Hebraic Section of the African and Middle Eastern Division has the first book published in Portugal, Moses ben Nahman's *Perush ha-Torah* (Lisbon, 1489).

One of the unique documents housed in the Rare Book and Special Collections Division is the Trevisan Codex, a highly prized manuscript forming part of the John Boyd Thacher collection and constituting the 1502 report by a Venetian agent in Spain of Spanish explorations in America and Portugal's arrival in Brazil and Calicut (on the Indian coast). A collection of manuscripts and printed books dealing with the exploits of Sir Francis Drake in America and Europe was a gift in 1979 from Hans P. Kraus. Among other valuable items, this collection contains sixteenth-century manuscript descriptions of the coasts of Central America, of the greater part of the Viceroyalty of Peru, of Francisco de Ulloa's 1553 expedition through the Straits of Magellan, and of the exploits of Nunho da Silva who, captured by Drake in 1577, became part of his command and later explored the Pacific coast of South America.

The Manuscript Division possesses outstanding Luso-Hispanic items including Columbus's 1502 manuscript book of privileges on vellum. That Division additionally holds several major groups of Hispanic and Portuguese materials, such as a collection of Portuguese manuscripts, the Hans P. Kraus Collection of Spanish Manuscripts, the Edward Harkness Collection, and the Henry Albert Monday Collection of Mexican colonial materials.

Important groups of materials can be found in the Law Library, the Hispanic

Page. Moses ben Nahman. Perush ha-Torah. Lisbon, 1489. The first book printed in any language in Portugal's capital city, Lisbon, was the Hebrew book, the *Commentary of the Pentateuch.* It was published only three years before the expulsion of the Jews from Spain and eight years before their removal from Portugal. *(Hebraic Section, African and Middle Eastern Division)*

Division, the Music Division, the Prints and Photographs Division, the Motion Picture, Broadcasting, and Recorded Sound Division, the Geography and Map Division, the Serial and Government Publications Division, the Microform Reading Room, the African and Middle Eastern Division, the American Folklife Reading Room, and the general collections of the Library of Congress. An outstanding strength of the Library's collections lie in the accumulation of printed materials from and on the areas of the Luso-Hispanic world. For practically two centuries, the Library has obtained complete sets of official gazettes, debates of parliamentary bodies, and all other significant official publications of national agencies, as well as selected provincial or state imprints. As a result, its collections of official documents are among the strongest in the world, as are its holdings of newspapers from Latin America, Spain, and Portugal. Microform copies of more than 4,000 pre-1800 Latin American imprints selected from the bibliographies of José Toribio Medina, Organization of American States's technical reports, and 8,179 nineteenth century Spanish plays are part of a rich body of research materials copied from other archives and collections.

As an integral part of these large and expanding collections, since 1942 the Library, through the Hispanic Division, has developed the ARCHIVE OF HISPANIC LITERATURE ON TAPE. The ARCHIVE today contains the recordings of more than 650 authors reading from their own works; eight of them have been awarded the Nobel Prize for Literature thus far.

Although most published Hispanic and Portuguese materials are located in the general collections and other special collections in the Library, bibliographic activity and reference services are conducted primarily in the Hispanic Division. In addition to special bibliographies and guides, the Hispanic Division prepares the annual, annotated *Handbook of Latin American Studies*. First published in 1936, the *Handbook* is universally recognized by scholars as the basic reference and acquisitions tool on Latin America. This long-term cooperative enterprise, which has more than a hundred contributing editors, each a noted specialist, effectively allows the Library's Latin American materials and its specialists to interact with others in the field, for purposes of research, collection development, and advancement of scholarship, and it is used by librarians to gauge the quality of their collections.

The primary function of the Hispanic Division continues to be the development of the Library's Hispanic and Portuguese collections, the facilitation of its use by the Congress of the United States, other federal agencies, and scholars, and the explanation and interpretation of its nature and content through published guides, bibliographies, and studies.

OPPOSITE. *First page of the letter written by Fray Bartolomé de Las Casas to King Charles I shortly before he left Spain for America. 1542.* Las Casas is known as a champion of the rights of native Americans. In this document, he presented a petition to help enforce new laws for America enacted in Spain in 1542. Through it he presented arguments to the Spanish governing body, the *Consejo de las Indias*, regarding the conduct of the religious orders concerning the issues of slavery, death, and rampant disregard for native life. We are also indebted to the friar for preserving the only record of Columbus's journal of his 1492–93 voyage, an abstract prepared in the early sixteenth century of which the Library of Congress holds a photographic copy in the Manuscript Division. *(Hans P. Kraus Collection, Manuscript Division)*

fray bartolome delas Casas electo obispo por v. m. dela ciudad real de chiapa besa
las manos a v. m. y dize q̃ pues q̃ por el real conseio delas yndias para
se despachar por q̃ asi conviene al serviçio de v. m. q̃ por q̃ el pueda mejor en
su offiçio hazer lo q̃ deve y servir a v. m. cumpliendo su real volutad
en la conservaçion delos yndios q̃ ya estan reduzidos ala corona real y asu
conversion y salvaçion y en la paçificaçion y reduçion delos q̃ no estan
paçificados ny reduzidos en la predicaçion del evangelio por a q̃llas gentes
y ytas comarcanas de aq̃l obispado y poblaçion tabien de españoles
q̃ el desea mucho onesta y hazer en la qual es grade el serviçio
v. m. resçibira a v. m. suplica sea servido de madarle hazer md
y proveer le delas cosas siguientes.

Primeramente q̃ v. m. sea servido de madar
señalar los limites de dho obispado y como
se distingua delos obispados de guatimala y hon
duras y tascala y guaxaca.

q̃ las provincias de guerra q̃ se llama teçulutla y la
razon esta el y sus compañeros an trabajado
de asegurar y traer de paz estan muy propinquas
ala dha ciudad y provincia de chiapa entre
dentro delos limites desu diocesi pues esta fue la
principal causa por la qual aceptó a q̃l obispado
conviene a saber por poder mejor proseguir
y effectuar la paçificaçion y conversion delas
gentes dellas y q̃ estas llegue hasta el golfo
dulce inclusive en la ysla de yucatan

y provision para el audiencia real y para todas las otras justicias
çelas y nros q̃ pertenecieren ala jurisdiçion en la
justiçia las justiçias reales den nro favor y
ayuda y execuçten nro lo q̃ el obispo les requi
riere y pidiere auxilio del braço seglar se
gun esta determinado de derecho y esto so pena.

y provision para la audiencia real y para todas las
otras justicias q̃ guarden inviolable mente las
immunidades ecclesias encomendadas y por todo segun
esta establecido por derecho poniendo penas de
quien el contrario hiziere o las q̃ bastaren

y ~~que dar~~ ~~que es de~~ ~~çertar~~

Literature and Philosophy

The LIBRARY OF CONGRESS possesses extensive holdings in Hispanic and Portuguese literature and philosophy. The literature collection provides a wide range of published works for the researcher, from the earliest printed materials in the United States and abroad to present-day publications. Highlighting the collection are the holdings in the ARCHIVE OF HISPANIC LITERATURE ON TAPE, the extensive collection of poetry and prose for the vast period of literary output from the works of Cervantes to the "boom" writers of Latin America, the materials related to Nobel Prize recipients, and works of philosophy.

The ARCHIVE OF HISPANIC LITERATURE ON TAPE is an evolving repository of poetry and prose recordings by Luso-Hispanic literary figures, from the 1940s to the present, located in the Hispanic Division. The collection began in 1942 when the noted Uruguayan poet Emilio Oribe read a poem dedicated to Archibald MacLeish in the Library of Congress Recording Laboratory. Largely with generous monetary grants provided by the Rockefeller Foundation from 1958 to 1961, the archive was expanded to include recordings made abroad expressly for the collection. This unique collection contains tape recordings of well over 650 writers reading selections from their own works in Spanish, Portuguese, Catalan, French, Quechua, Náhuatl, English, Guarani, and Zapotec, as well as accompanying interviews and commentaries.

Practically all of the outstanding literary figures and outstanding writers from the Caribbean and numerous Hispanic and Portuguese authors, as well as Hispanic American writers of the past fifty years are represented. Several Nobel Prize recipients appear, including Gabriela Mistral and Pablo Neruda (Chile), Miguel Angel Asturias (Guatemala), Vicente Aleixandre, Juan Ramón Jiménez, and Camilo José Cela (Spain), Gabriel García Márquez (Colombia), Octavio Paz (Mexico), and many other famous writers, such as José Luis Borges, Carlos Drummond de Andrade, bibliophile José E. Mindlin, Mario Vargas Llosa, Jorge Amado, and Rachel de Queiroz.

The ARCHIVE contains documentation of distinctive regional dialects and speech patterns and of social criticism voiced by many writers. The noted Spanish author Juan Goytisolo penned an obituary of Francisco Franco on the day that the Spanish ruler died. The following day he recorded it for the ARCHIVE OF HISPANIC LITERATURE ON TAPE, during his visit to the Library of Congress, before anyone else had a chance to read it. Reference tapes for the collection are housed in the Hispanic Division, with supplemental notebooks containing lists and texts of the selections read. A published guide describes the collection, providing biographic and bibliographic information on each writer in the ARCHIVE at the time of the publication.

OPPOSITE. *"Calavera Don Quijote y Sancho Panza" ca. 1905. José Guadalupe Posada. Monografía. Las obras de José Guadalupe Posada, grabador mexicano, con introducción de Diego Rivera. Mexico, Mexican folkways, 1930.* The noted Mexican artist Posada, during a very creative life, devoted his energies to producing works of satire of contemporary figures, especially politicians, and translating legendary figures into a world of skeletons and skulls. Posada's drawings paralleled the revolutionary awakening that would transform Mexican art as well as its politics. Additional original works and even printing plates of Posada are found in the Library's Prints and Photographs Division. Posada's calavera of Don Quixote is one of his best prints, displaying prodigious movement. The work clearly shows that even noted literary works were not spared the pen of the Mexican artist. *(Rosenwald Collection, Rare Book and Special Collections Division)*

Pablo Neruda. Photograph. [1966]. For over two decades the Chilean Pablo Neruda was one of the most-quoted poets in the Spanish language, for whom admiration amounted to worship and disapproval to excoriation. In 1971 he was awarded the Nobel Prize in Literature; he died in the fall of 1973 in Santiago, Chile. He is pictured here during his recording session in the Library of Congress on June 20, 1966. *(Archive of Hispanic Literature on Tape, Hispanic Division)*

The poetry and prose collection of Latin America's first Nobel Prize for literature recipient, Gabriela Mistral, is found in the Manuscript Division on more than twenty-five reels of microfilm. Mistral is representative of the numerous Luso-Hispanic authors who have become highly acclaimed as regional and world class writers.

The still expanding collection of works by Miguel de Cervantes Saavedra (1547–1616), the most important writer of Renaissance Spain and one of the most eminent writers of world literature, reflects the sustained interest of the scholarly community in his work. Nearly a thousand examples of his literary output are listed in *Works by Miguel de Cervantes Saavedra in the Library of Congress* (1994), including translations of his work into thirty-three languages including Bulgarian, Chinese, Lithuanian, Marathi, Norwegian, Oriya, Tajik, and Uzbek. In addition to copies of his works in Thomas Jefferson's collection, the Library's holdings are enhanced by twentieth-century donations from Leonard Kebler, found now in the Rare Book and Special Collections Division.

The tradition of epic poetry in the Hapsburg period, which influenced later forms of prose chronicle and narrative and political verse, is highlighted by the outstanding 1597 edition of Alonso de Ercilla's *La Araucana* (regarding Spanish conflict with the native peoples of Chile) and the 1589 edition of Juan de Castellanos narrative poem *Primera parte de las elegías de varones illustres de indias*, both located in the Rare Book and Special Collections Division.

Over 8,100 Spanish plays, published in the late nineteenth and early twentieth centuries, were received from the Hispanic Society of America in 1938 shortly before the opening of the Hispanic Division. This SPANISH PLAY COLLECTION (now on 161 reels of microfilm in the Microform Reading Room) contains works published principally in Madrid and Barcelona after 1850 and includes those by lesser-known Spanish authors and regional pieces in Catalan and Galician. Drama, comedy, and *zarzuela* (musicals) are well represented. Among the authors in this collection are Carlos Arniches y Bamera, Joaquin Dicenta Benedicto, Antonio García Gutiérrez, Antonio Gil y Zarate, and Ricardo de la Vega.

Complementing this collection is the SPANISH DRAMA OF THE GOLDEN AGE: THE COMEDIA COLLECTION IN THE UNIVERSITY OF PENNSYLVANIA LIBRARIES COLLECTION (on eighty-six reels of microfilm in the Microform Reading Room). It contains nearly three thousand early editions by more than two hundred

Spanish Golden Age authors, including Calderón de la Barca, Cervantes, Gongora, Lope de Vega, Pérez de Montalvan, Roja Zorrilla, Mira de Americua, Moneto y Cabanar, Gabriel Tellez, Velez de Guevara, Zamora, and Lope de Rueda.

The Rare Book and Special Collections Division houses the REPOSITORIO CAMONEANO assembled by Carlos da Silva and published in 1880–1881. The collection comprises monographs, periodicals, newspaper literature, manuscripts, catalogs, and clippings gathered in honor of the tercentenary of the Portuguese poet Luis de Camões.

The PORTUGUESE MANUSCRIPTS COLLECTION was purchased in 1927 and 1929. It is part of the nucleus of the Library of Congress's collections in Portuguese history and literature and is an important group of documents in the Manuscript and in the Rare Book and Special Collections Divisions. The Archive of Folk Culture, in the American Folklife Reading Room, houses a large collection of *literatura de cordel*, ephemeral chapbooks, small books containing ballads, tales or tracts, found in northeastern Brazil. The Library of Congress's holdings of this unique material, initiated by Sol Biderman, has swollen to well over five thousand items.

Researchers have at their disposal comprehensive literature bibliographies and such vital reference works as the editions of Antonio Palau y Dulcet's *Manual del Librero Hispano-Americano*, the most important work on Luso-Hispanic publishing. The Library has the *Seminario Erudito* of Antonio de Valladares y Sotomayor and Juan Semper y Guarinos's four-volume *Biblioteca económico-política* (Madrid 1801–1821) and his six-volume *Ensayo de una biblioteca española de los mejores escritores del reynado de Carlos III* (Madrid 1785–1789).

The ideas of the twentieth-century Spanish philosopher José Ortega y Gasset are found in a massive eighty-two-reel microfilm collection (in the Manuscript Division) of his manuscripts, notes, and correspondence. In the late 1970s the Hispanic Division worked directly with the Ortega Foundation (Madrid) to develop a preservation copy microfilm of the Ortega y Gasset Archive, helping to arrange the original materials in the process. José Ortega y Gasset, author of such works as *España invertebrada* (1922) and *La rebelión de las masas* (1929), was Spain's best known contemporary philosopher. General works in the Library on natural philosophy range from Fray Vicente de Burgos's *El libro de proprietatibus rerum* (Toulouse, 1494) and Alvaro Gutiérez de Torres's very early encyclopedia of natural history *El sumario de las maravillosas y espantables cosas que en el mundo han acontescido* (1524), in the Rare Book and Special Collections Division, and works by Bartolomé de las Casas and Juan de Zumárraga in the Manuscript Division, to recent publications on liberation theology, Umbanda, and the Opus Dei in the general

Gabriela Mistral. Photograph. [1950s]. The Chilean poet Gabriela Mistral holds the distinction of being the first Hispanic American to be awarded the Nobel Prize for Literature, conferred upon her in Stockholm on November 15, 1945. She established residence in New York City in the 1950s and served as the Chilean delegate to the United Nations Commission on the Status of Women until her death on January 10, 1957. In addition to her recordings and printed works, a large microform collection of her personal papers is located in the Library's Manuscript Division. *(Archive of Hispanic Literature on Tape, Hispanic Division)*

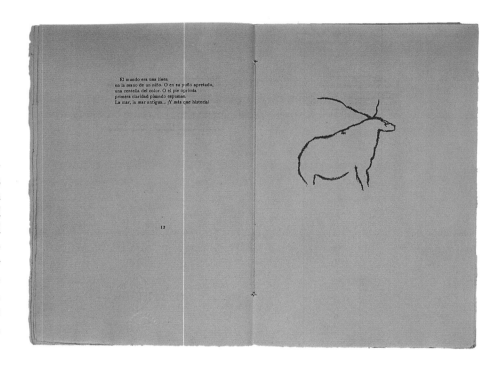

Picasso, con pinturas ineditas de la cueva de Nerja.
Vicente Aleixandre. Malaga, El Guadalhorce,
1961. The Nobel Prize-recipient Spanish poet, Vicente Aleixandre, and the noted Spanish artist Pablo Picasso collaborated with their creative genius to provide simple reflections on the incredibly significant paleolithic period cave drawings found near Nerja, Malaga, Spain. Aleixandre recorded for the Library's Archive of Hispanic Literature on Tape. *(Rare Book and Special Collections Division)*

collections of the Library of Congress, and other conflicting philosophies of social movements in the Luso-Hispanic world.

The SERIE CONFLICTO RELIGIOSO (from Mexico's Instituto Nacional de Antropología e Historia/INAH) is a fifty-two-reel microfilm collection of twentieth-century printed and manuscript materials on the social history of Catholicism in Mexico. Located in the Microform Reading Room, this collection contains speeches, correspondence, books, pamphlets, historical studies, minutes, newspaper and magazine articles, memoirs, reports, and bulletins addressing social, political, and military history, the founding of the Knights of Columbus in Mexico, the Cristero movement, sexual education, relations with the United States, and organized labor. From the writings of the fifteenth and sixteenth centuries on millenarianism and utopianism exacerbated by Europe's initial introduction to American societies to the more modern period, in which social reformers experimented with positivism, socialism, anarchism, and the thinking of the Peruvian *Sendero Luminoso*, opportunities abound for rewarding research in literary and philosophical studies.

Adoration of the Magi. Juan de Torquemada. Meditationes seu Contemplationes devotissimae. Mainz 1479. The three magi in this illustration from a devotional book of 1479 suggest the opulence and splendor of African and Asian potentates as imagined by Europeans of the late Middle Ages. Born in Valladolid, Cardinal Juan de Torquemada (1388–1468), one of the great intellects of the Catholic Church in the fifteenth century and named the Defender of the Faith by Pope Eugene IV in 1437, was a strong defender of Renaissance artists. He introduced printing to Italy. The Dominican Juan de Torquemada is not to be confused with Tomás de Torquemada, the Inquisitor General of Spain. *(Rosenwald Collection, Rare Book and Special Collections Division)*

The Arts

OPPOSITE. *Introductory page. Antiphonary [choir book]. Spain. Black, red, and blue ink on vellum. Early sixteenth century.* Antiphons are chant melodies usually sung before and after a psalm verse and are performed by the alternate singing of two singers or choirs. This page contains musical notations and text from the choir part for the celebration of the feast of Saint Andrew. Elaborately decorated liturgical manuscripts (Bibles, Missals, Books of Hours) have a long tradition in medieval and Renaissance Europe. The border design of this work, with its emphasis on repetition and fluid calligraphic swirls, seems to rely on an Islamic decorative tradition rooted in the visual arts and architecture. The mental world of early modern Spain, although dominated by the Roman Catholic Church, included Islamic and Jewish features as well. *(Music Division)*

AN EXTRAORDINARY MANUSCRIPT ANTIPHONARY on vellum from early sixteenth century Spain reflecting both the Latin Mass and the enduring survival of Islamic thought and aesthetics through a decorative tradition rooted in the visual arts and architecture is part of the magnificent collections of Hispanic and Portuguese materials on the arts and music in the Library of Congress. Equally stunning is a 1576 edition, published by Pedro Ocharte in Mexico, of a *graduale dominicale*, the Library of Congress's earliest American music imprint. That musical score, given by the Friends of Music of the Library of Congress in 1940, is part of a rich body of materials which include a 1564 *Psalterium* published in Seville and the Mexican manuscript *Misa pro defunctis* by Francisco Guerrero, the eminent sixteenth-century Spanish composer.

From the early sixteenth-century vellum antiphonary to remarkable examples of modern architecture in the Luso-Hispanic world, the Library of Congress possesses unparalleled art materials from its diverse general and special collections. Through these documents, one is able to study in detail a particular period or compare many periods and genres of cultural expression. The Library's historical record of music from the Luso-Hispanic world is complemented by materials in the Music Division from more contemporary composers and artists. In the Music Division are found the printed and manuscript compositions of the Brazilian composer Alberto Nepomuceno; in the KOUSSEVITZKY ARCHIVE OF MUSICAL MANUSCRIPTS is found Heitor Villa-Lobos's Symphony no. 11; and correspondence of Pablo Casals is in the CHARLES MARTIN TORNOV LOEFFLER COLLECTION. The Library of Congress received a major bequest of compositions, letters, and photographs from Mario Castelnuovo-Tedesco (1895–1968), in the Music Division, which included holdings pertaining to Isaac Albeñiz (1860–1909), Pablo Casals (1876–1973), Manuel de Falla (1876–1916), Cristobal Halffter Jiménez (1930–), Federico García Lorca (1898–1936), Josep María Mestres-Quadreny 1929–), Frederico Mompow (1893–1989), Joaquin Nin (1879–1949), Luis de Pablo (1930–), and Andrés Segovia (1893–1987).

The comprehensive LAURO AYESTARAN COLLECTION, in the Music Division, is a 6100- item collection of all music published in Uruguay, and music published outside of the country by Uruguayan composers. Genres represented in the collection include concert, theater, dance, popular, and folk music in printed and manuscript forms, published from the mid-nineteenth century to the 1960s.

The Recorded Sound Reference Center of the Motion Picture, Broadcasting, and Recorded Sound Division has substantial holdings of Hispanic and Portuguese classical, popular, and folk recordings. More than two hundred

Folio. *Graduale Dominicale, secudum normam Missalis noui: exdecreto Sancti* Concilij Triden denuo. *Mexico, Pedro Ocharte, 1576.* Received by the Music Division in 1940 as a gift from the Friends of Music in the Library of Congress, the *Graduale Dominicale* is the first sixteenth-century American musical imprint in the collections, the second edition of the 1571 original of the same title. Earlier, Bishop Juan de Zumárraga, first Bishop in Mexico in 1528, was instrumental in the introduction of the printing press into the Spanish American colonies. At his insistence, Juan Cromberger established a branch of his Sevillian publishing house in Mexico City and shipped to America all the equipment and supplies vital to its operation. Juan Pablos, of Brescia, Italy, became Cromberger's Mexican agent and later the owner of the press on which he printed the 1539 edition of the *Breve y más compendiosa doctrina christiana en lengua mexicana y castellana*, the first American book. The 1544 edition, the earliest example of a book printed by Pablos's press in American collections, is found in the Library of Congress's Rare Book and Special Collections Division. *(Music Division)*

recordings of Villa-Lobos and nearly fifty by Ginastera appear, along with contemporary recordings by Chicana singer Lydia Mendoza.

Among the items in the DAYTON C. MILLER FLUTE COLLECTION—a collection of flutes and books, manuscripts, music, and pictorial material relating to the flute's history and performance in the Music Division—are pre-Columbian Guatemalan and Peruvian whistles and flutes.

Over the years, numerous concerts of Luso-Hispanic music have been presented in the Library of Congress, including performances of *Las Cantigas de Santa María* by the Waverly Consort; solo performances by Brazilian pianist Arthur Moreira Lima, by pianist Frederick Marvin in honor of the 200th anniversary of the death of Padre Antonio Soler y Ramos, Spanish guitarist Josep Joan Henríquez, pianist Janet Ahlquist of eighteenth- and twentieth-century Portuguese compositions, Spanish pianist Antonio Baciero of Spanish baroque music, and Mexican ethnomusicologist Antonio Zepeda of pre-Columbian music; and outdoor concerts of *jarocho*, Puerto Rican, mambo, *cumbia*, and other Luso-Hispanic and Caribbean folk music through the American Folklife Center's program.

Documentation of culture through photographic and print form is well represented in the Library of Congress. The ARCHIVE OF HISPANIC CULTURE is a photographic reference collection for the study of Latin American art and architecture in the Prints and Photographs Division, initially funded by the Rockefeller Foundation. The collection illustrates indigenous art works dating from the colonial period through the twentieth century in Latin America and artistically influential Hispanic and Portuguese monuments in Spain, Portugal, the Philippines, and the United States. Over the years the ARCHIVE has amassed some 19,000 photographs, 3,200 color slides, and 2,500 negatives from the 1880s to the 1940s.

The ARCHIVE focuses on Latin American architecture (ecclesiastical and civil, particularly from Mexico and Brazil), painting (photocopies of colonial religious paintings, *santos*, portraits, and modern Mexican murals), sculpture (some pre-Columbian and modern, mostly colonial religious sculpture from Ecuador), graphic arts (photos of sixteenth-century codices, nineteenth-century engravings, lithographs, genre prints, modern etchings, woodcuts, and posters), minor arts (textile, furniture, jewelry, and ceramics) and general scenes of Latin America. The ARCHIVE also comprises a large postcard collection containing excellent scenes of late nineteenth- and early twentieth-century daily life, by country.

The MEXICAN INDIAN PICTORIAL DOCUMENTS COLLECTION, in the Prints and Photographs Division, has substantial photographic reproductions of original pre- and post-contact indigenous records, including *codices*, related to Meso

Ribeiro House, Largo do Boticário, Rio de Janeiro, Brazil. [1940]. Black and white photograph. The Archive of Hispanic Culture is replete with examples of the art and architecture of historical and contemporary Luso-Hispanic America. Many of the reproductions serve to illustrate the relationship of the structure to the environment, as this photograph vividly reveals. Among noteworthy examples in the Archive are the works of the newly emerging architects of the Americas, e.g., Oscar Niemeyer, in the immediate pre- and post-World War II period. (*Archive of Hispanic Culture, Prints and Photographs Division*)

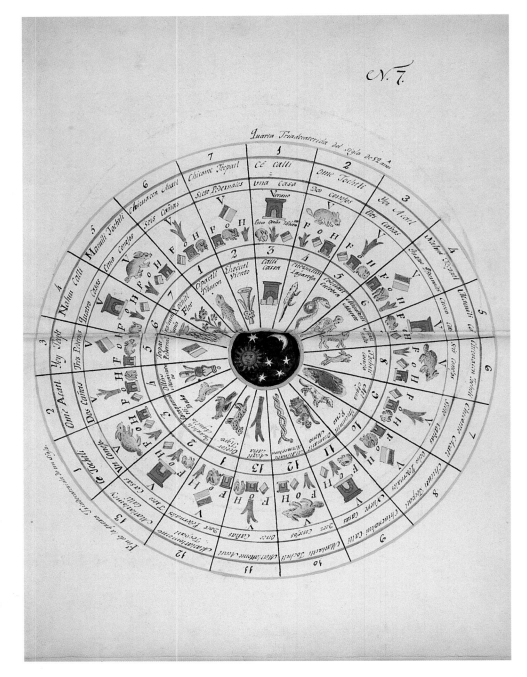

Calendar wheel, no. 7. In Mariano Fernández Echeverría y Veytia. Historia del orígen de las gentes que poblaron la America septentrional. [early 19th-century manuscript facsimile]. The *tonalpohualli,* or sacred calendar, ruled the life of each Mexica (Aztec) and was consulted on all important occasions. It was made up of 260 days, or 13 months of 20 days. The inner portions of this calendar represent the symbols for the 20 days and the sun, moon, and stars. Death in 1780 cut short Echeverría y Veytia's effort to complete a study of the calendars used in Mexico before the early sixteenth-century Spanish conquest. A manuscript copy of his original work (which included the illustration of seven Mexica calendar wheels) in the Real Academia de la Historia in Madrid was prepared early in the nineteenth century and entered the Library of Congress through the acquisition of the Peter Force Collection in 1867. *(Peter Force Collection, Manuscript Division)*

American Indian cultures. These reproductions were collected by John B. Glass during his participation in the preparation of the multivolume *Handbook of Middle American Indians.*

The Prints and Photographs Division's GUDIOL COLLECTION consists of about 1,750 photoprints of Spanish architecture, paintings, and sculpture from the Middle Ages to the twentieth century. Prints by Goya and Picasso and the Salvadorean Toño Salazar's and Mexican Miguel Covarrubias's collections are found in that Division's fine prints collection. In the LESSING J. ROSENWALD COLLECTION in the Rare Book and Special Collections Division is an outstanding selection of *livre d'artiste,* a type developed in France during the first quarter of the twentieth century that spread throughout Europe. These limited editions contained special illustrations, in many cases signed by noted contemporary artists. Works illustrated by Pablo Picasso, Maurice Utrillo, Salvador Dalí, Joan Miró, Juan Gris, and Oscar Domínguez, among others, are found in that collection.

The HISTORICAL PRINTS COLLECTION, in the Prints and Photographs Division, includes pre-twentieth-century lithographs, engravings, and other illustrations of Latin America, Spain, and Portugal, as well as items on such topics as Christopher Columbus, Discovery and Exploration, Indians, Mexican War, Spanish American War, and the Punitive Expedition Against Pancho Villa. A

Courret Hermanos, Fotografos. Gaucho of the Argentine Republic. Albumen silver print, 1868 in Recuerdos del Peru. Lot 4831 H Vol. 1, Plate 50. This photograph of an Argentine gaucho was included in a two-volume souvenir album, *Recuerdos del Peru,* prepared by the Lima firm of Courret Hermanos. The album contains several views of Lima, Arequipa, Callao, Arica, La Paz, and portraits of muleteers, bullfighters, Andean Indian peoples, and a gaucho. The photographs contained in the album and other photographic collections for the Luso-Hispanic world from the nineteenth and twentieth centuries provide an added dimension in the understanding of these cultures. *(Prints and Photographs Division)*

fascinating collection of stereographs contains views of Latin American daily life for the period 1875 to 1920, and the poster collection in the Prints and Photographs Division addresses political and many other themes from Argentina, Brazil, Cuba, Chile, Mexico, Puerto Rico, and Spain.

Invaluable photographic collections in the Prints and Photographs Division, both from the point of view of the art of photography as well as of cultural expression, reinforce resources on the Luso-Hispanic world found throughout the Library. A very brief listing of such gems includes forty Mathew B. Brady photographs of the first Pan American conference in Washington (1889–1890); the William Howard Taft collection from his 1907 trip to Panama, Cuba, and Puerto Rico; the John Pershing photographic collection relating to his 1916 Mexican Punitive Expedition and his subsequent Latin American travels; the Josephus Daniels collection of more than six thousand photographs from his 1933–1941 ambassadorship in Mexico; the Hovey collection of 100 photos of Peruvian and other southern South American views (1868); the Depaz and Moreau collection of sixteen views of late nineteenth century village life and operations of St. James sugar plantation in Martinique; the Escudero y Arias collection of nearly two hundred *carte-de-visite* photographs of major figures and events in 1850–1880 Mexico, including photographs of Maximilian's execution in 1867; the Detroit Publishing photographic collection of 1885–1914 Mexico and the Caribbean, including 125 photographs of the Spanish American War; the Shaw collection of twenty photographs of Panama (1884–1885); the Milhollen collection of fifty Peruvian photographs (1895–1905); the Archambault collection of photographs of Nicaraguan Canal construction and related street scenes 1899–1900; the Cuban Department of Public Works collection of 225 photographs of road conditions and buildings in Cuba 1907–1908; the Leland Harrison collection of photographs taken during his post-World War I tour of duty as Ambassador to Colombia; the William Henry Jackson collection of photographs of the West Indies, the Bahamas, Venezuela 1900–1905, and Mexico 1884–1885; and a collection of some 124 photographs of the United Fruit Company's Central American operations, primarily for 1948 but including items from 1876–1936, are indicative of the variety of themes in the Library's photographic collections. Many more photographic collections related to nineteenth- and twentieth-century Latin American living conditions and architecture, the Spanish American War, interoceanic canal construction, the Cuban missile crisis, the Spanish Civil War, and many other subjects are found in the Prints and Photographs Division.

The Bottom of Gatun Lock – Panama Canal

J. Pennell

Joseph Pennell. The Bottom of Gatun Lock. Lithograph, 1912. Panama Canal Series. The history surrounding the completion of the Panama Canal in 1914 and various nineteenth century Isthmian Canal ventures is richly represented in the collections of the Library of Congress. Pennell's classic works record the crucial moments when the grandeur of canal construction ushered in a unique age of U.S. engineering prowess. *(Gift of Joseph and Elizabeth Robins Pennell, Prints and Photographs Division)*

The Library of Congress has collected early recordings of indigenous peoples. Carl Lumholtz's 1898 recording of the Huichol peoples in Mexico is found in the HELEN H. ROBERTS COLLECTION of ethnomusicological field recordings in the Archive of Folk Song, along with Roberts's own 1920s and 1930s recordings done in Jamaica.

Ethnomusicologist Henrietta Yurchenco has been responsible for large portions of Luso-Hispanic folk recordings now in the Library of Congress. Her collection in the Archive of Folk Song contains field recordings of Mexican and Guatemalan Indian music and field recordings of the traditional ballads, wedding songs, and stories sung by Sephardic Jews made in Spain and Morocco in 1954 and 1956. Following her 1942 recording expedition among Mexico's Tarascan Indians, Dr. Yurchenco was employed by the Library of Congress, the Inter-American Indian Institute, and the Mexican Department of Education to document the music of some of the most isolated Indian communities of Mexico and Guatemala. She recorded from 1944 to 1946 the Seri and Yaqui of the state of Sonora, the Tarahumara of Chihuahua, the Cora of Nayarit, the Huichol of Jalisco, the Tzotzil Maya and Tzeltal Maya of Chiapas, and the Quiché, Kekchi, and Ixil of Guatemala. Aside from the hunting kivee and the war songs of the Seri, the resulting 151-disc collection primarily consists of vocal and instrumental music from religious festivals and rituals performed on both indigenous and European instruments. The Archive of Folk Culture contains recordings of Mexican indigenous and European music as well as music from Brazil, Chile, Colombia, Cuba, Haiti, Panama, Peru, Puerto Rico, Surinam, Trinidad, and Luso-Hispanics in the United States.

The Motion Picture, Broadcasting, and Recorded Sound Division possesses copies of rare Mexican and Argentine silent films, feature motion pictures by major Hispanic and Portuguese directors, including Luís Buñuel, and numerous commercial films produced by Latin American subsidiaries of Hollywood studios (Columbia and RKO). Over fifty feature-length movies from Mexico, the earliest from 1933, are in the collection, including *Juárez y Maximiliano* (1933), *Flor de caña* (1948), and *Pulgarcito* (1958).

Complementing these special collections are the extensive general book holdings which provide coverage of every period and geographical location of Luso-Hispanic culture. Use of the various guides to these materials, such as the annual *Handbook of Latin American Studies* compiled in the Hispanic Division, and consultations with reference specialists in the Hispanic Division and in the other special collections of the Library will increase access to this rich body of material.

OPPOSITE. *Idol at Copan. In Frederick Catherwood. Detail. View of Ancient Monuments in Central America, Chiapas, and Yucatan. New York, 1844.* The rich architecture and writing of the Mayan peoples of Central America and Mexico were captured in the nineteenth-century lithographic prints of John Stephens and Frederick Catherwood, who visited the sites. Mayan culture rivaled that of the Incas and Mexicas (Aztecs); however, its period of prominence predated late fifteenth-century contact with Europe. Currently, a number of exciting developments in the deciphering of the Mayan language are stimulating heightened interest in the study of Mayan societies. *(Rare Book and Special Collections Division)*

The Hispanic and Portuguese World

Spain and Portugal occupy the Iberian Peninsula, which is separated at its southern tip from North Africa by only a narrow strait situated at the juncture of the Mediterranean and the Atlantic. This key geographical position played an important part in Iberia's history. From ancient times various Mediterranean civilizations came, attracted by mineral and agricultural potential. The Romans had the most lasting impact. By the second century A.D. most of Iberia had been romanized in language, religion, and law.

From the early eighth century until the late fifteenth century Iberia's history was Muslim domination and the Christian attempts to reclaim political control over the peninsula. By the fifteenth century a stable monarchy provided the impetus for early Portuguese expansion. In Spain, the marriage of Isabel and Fernando in 1479 marked the first steps towards forging modern Spain. From those events, the modern states of Spain and Portugal emerged. Portugal became the earliest European state.

And it is the emigrants to America from this geographically unified but culturally very diverse Iberian Peninsula who, in the fifteenth and sixteenth centuries, carried with them their experiences, culture, and expectations of what they could accomplish to America. In these new surroundings they were forced to adjust to a context quite different from that of Spain and Portugal. Ibero-American societies began to take shape in part as a result of the adaptations that Iberian emigrants made to the new situation they found. The indigenous peoples, with whom they mingled, constituted yet another crucial factor in the equation that produced American societies. The Library of Congress's extensive Luso-Hispanic collections provide ample information about the centuries of human existence on the Iberian Peninsula and its influences throughout the world.

The Spanish and Portuguese monarchies reached the zenith of their power during the time when printing was revolutionizing the consciousness of the Western world. Both Spain and Portugal had extended the frontiers of European control outside Europe, particularly by spreading the use of printing. The emerging art of printing chronicles the period of Iberia's greatest power and wealth; it illustrates how the world and its European rivals felt Iberia's impact.

The manuscript and book catalogs of the Biblioteca Nacional, Madrid, are available in the Library of Congress, such as Antonio Paz y Melía's *Papeles de Inquisición . . .* (1947) and, notably, the colossal *Inventario General de Manuscritos*, which has been appearing since 1933. The more than 4,800-microfiche *Catálogo general de libros impresos*, in the Microform Reading Room, provides a comprehensive record of authors and works in Spain's Biblioteca Nacional up to 1987. Also present are

OPPOSITE. *Hispalis [Seville]. In Georg Braun and Francis Hogenberg. Civitates orbis terrarum. Cologne, 1612–18. vol. 5/6.* In this plate, the Netherlandish artist, Georg Hoefnagel, portrays Seville frontally from a raised perspective. By 1580 Seville, with more than 130,000 inhabitants, was the largest city of Spain. It has a long, prominent history from Roman, Islamic, and medieval times. Its wealth and prestige grew rapidly toward the end of the fifteenth century due to Columbus's explorations and Spanish colonization of America. In 1503, the House of Trade, *la Casa de Contratación*, was founded in the city, assuring Seville's control over commerce and trade with America. Seville is the location of the important General Archive of the Indies, which contains the administrative papers of Spain's overseas colonies. *(Geography and Map Division)*

Occidens

Septentrio

SEVILLA

Que non ha vissto

non ha vissto maravilla

A Quemadero.
B Nuestre señora de abadia.
C S.ª Elena. Cc Rio Tagarette.
D Fuente de Caliteros.
E Rio Guadalquivir.
F S. Juan del foracte.
G Huerte del orio.
H El Alcocer casa Real.
I La yglesia maior.
K El matadero. KK quartos.

L Santa Cruz. LL Castillo de dessa.
M S.ª Marina. Septilo.
N S.ª Agues ille.
O Camino de Carmona.
P Camino para granada.
Q S.ª Trinidad.
R Alcalaer.
S Execution de fusticia de los
    cornados potentes.
T Execucion d'alcaparcos publicos.

HISPALIS

Meridies

Oriens

D. NICOLAO MALEFART AMICO VETERI ET CONGERRONI HISPAENSI EPIDISSIMO GEORGIVS HOVFNAGLIVS AMICITIE MONVMETV D. AÑO CIƆ IƆ XCIII. FRANCOF. AD MOENVM

Portolan Chart of the Mediterranean World. Mateo Prunes [Majorca] 1559. Vellum. A cartographic revolution occurred in the Mediterranean world in the thirteenth century with the emergence of a new type of chart, the portolan chart. This coincided with the surge in seafaring activity and Atlantic exploration which began before the end of that century. The colorful one-of-a-kind portolan chart was drawn on vellum in 1559. Mapmaker Mateus Prunes (1532–1594) was a leading member of a family of Majorcan cartographers who lived and worked on that island from the early sixteenth to the late seventeenth centuries. The chart depicts the Mediterranean Sea, the Black Sea, part of the Red Sea, the Atlantic coast of Africa from Cape Spartel to Senegal, and the European coast to northern Scandinavia. Both real and mythical islands appear in the northwest. The real ones include Fixlanda (Iceland) and Isola Verde (probably Greenland). Among the mythical islands are Isola de Brazil and Isola de Maydi, the latter possibly a name of Arabic origin that first appeared on the 1325 chart by Angelino Dalorto. *(Vellum Chart Collection, Geography and Map Division)*

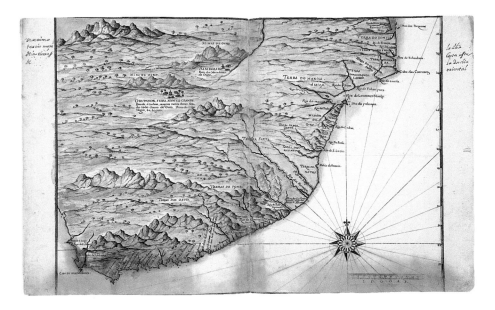

such research tools as Francisco Sintes Obrador's *Archivos y bibliotecas de España* (1953) and J. E. Martínez Ferrando's *Tres archivos de España* (1950), a guide to the Archives of the Corona de Aragón, Simancas, and Indias.

The work of prime concern for the study of Spain is the Real Academia de la Historia's famed 112-volume *Colección de documentos inéditos para la historia de España* (1842–1895), along with its six-volume *Colección de documentos para la historia de España y sus Indias* (1928–1934), *Documentos inéditos para la historia de España* (1936–1957), and the forty-seven-volume *Memorial histórico español: colección de documentos, opúsculos y antigüedades* (1851–1916, 1947–). These collections reproduce documents that are now either lost, in private hands, in the archive at Simancas, or original manuscripts of several chroniclers.

Another significant collection, the PORTUGUESE MANUSCRIPTS COLLECTION, purchased in 1927 and 1929, is part of a group of nearly 28,500 items—manuscripts and printed works related to Portuguese history and literature—14,000 items of which are in Portuguese. Like the book and pamphlet portions of the collection, the majority of the manuscripts, which span a period of more than five hundred years, are from the private libraries of the Conde de Olivais e Penha Longa and Antonio Augusto de Carvalho Monteiro.

Substantial items are concerned with Sebastianism, the belief that King

Sebastian, killed in North Africa in 1578, would return to restore Portugal to its former greatness; Luis de Camões (1524–1580), author of Portugal's epic poem *Os Lusíadas*; the military orders of knighthood; general historical works, histories of the Portuguese sovereigns, letters of seventeenth-century diplomatic figures, and a volume containing 210 letters (1774–1779) of Manoel de Cunha Menezes, captain general of Pernambuco and Bahia.

The PORTUGUESE PAMPHLETS COLLECTION 1610–1921, on seventy-five reels of microfilm in the Microform Reading Room, was collected primarily by Antonio Augusto de Carvalho Monteiro (1850–1920). It reflects the contemporary interests of nineteenth-century Portugal, including items on Camões, the Marques de Pombal, Brazil, dynastic struggles, voyages of discovery, political tracts, criticism of the monarchy and other officials, literary and intellectual polemics, eulogies, sermons, prose and poetry by Leite de Vasconcellos, and historical essays by Sousa Viterbo and Gabriel Pereira, as well as writings on agriculture, science, and music.

The LESSING J. ROSENWALD COLLECTION of illustrated books from the fifteenth through the twentieth centuries, in the Rare Book and Special Collections Division, contains numerous treasures of the Luso-Hispanic world. Along with the first book printed in the Philippines, *Doctrina Christiana, en lengua española y tagala* (1593), in this extraordinary collection are found a remarkable 1524 edition of *Praeclara Ferdinadi Cortesii de Nova maris Oceani Hyspania narratio*—Hernando Cortés's 1520 letter about Mexico to Charles V of Spain—, 1479 and 1484 editions of Juan de Torquemada's *Meditationes seu Contemplationes devotissimae*, and works by Rodrigo Sánchez de Arévalo, Fernando Mexía, Luis de Lucena, Enrique de Aragón, Pedro de Castrovol, Pedro de Cieza de León's *Parte primera dela Chronica del Peru* (1553), Francisco López de Gómara's *Primera y segunda parte dela historia general de las Indias* (1553), and Pedro Nuñes's 1537 translation of Sacrobosco's *Sphaera mundi*.

The VELLUM CHART COLLECTION, in the Geography and Map Division, contains twenty-seven rare nautical charts and six atlases on vellum from several major early schools of chart making, particularly from Spanish and Italian groups. With examples ranging from an anonymous fourteenth-century chart of the eastern Mediterranean and the Black Seas to the eighteenth- and early nineteenth-century hydrographic charts depicting portions of the Caribbean Sea from the Royal Naval School at Cádiz, the collection provides over four centuries of examples for the study of the development of navigational charts. The 1559 manuscript chart on vellum of the Mediterranean, Atlantic, and North Sea coastlines drawn by the Mallorcan Mateo Prunes and Battista Agnese's 1544 vellum atlas of the world—with particularly early representations of the Western Hemisphere and a chart depicting Magellan's circumnavigation of the globe in 1519–1522 and strikingly detailed information on the Mediterranean world—are vivid examples of the collection's stunning quality.

Additional cartographic works from throughout the period of Hispanic and Portuguese expansion can be found in the Geography and Map Division. Extensive examples of Portuguese colonial maps make the Library of Congress one of the largest centers for cartographic research on that empire. Among outstanding works are Armando Cortesão's six-volume *Portugaliae monumenta cartographica*, maps published by the Agencia Geral do Ultramar, such as the *Carta da Colônia da Guiné Portuguesa* (1889), the *Carta da Africa meridional portuguesa* (1886), the *Carta de Angola, contendo indicações de produção e salubridade* (1885), and the unique 1630 manuscript atlas, *Taboas geraes de toda a navegação divididas e emendadas por Dom Ieronimo de Attayde* by João Teixeira, cosmographer to the King of Portugal, which contains charts of Brazil, Africa, Southeast Asia, the Indian Ocean, the Americas, Europe, and the Mediterranean region. Teixeira's monumental work, which parallels Portuguese overseas efforts in the sixteenth and first half of the seventeenth centuries, was a major source of geographical information in the ongoing international rivalry between Portugal and Spain that had accelerated from the late fifteenth century. The provenance of the atlas is alone an interesting story. Spaniard Francisco de Seixas y Lovera (1650–1705/6), a Mexican viceroy, acquired the manuscript atlas from the Portuguese Royal Library and Archives "using intelligence and money." He presented this extremely valuable purchase to Spain's King Charles II (1661–1700) so that "his Majesty [could] use it in the Congresses against Portugal."

The OTTO VOLLBEHR COLLECTION of incunabula in the Rare Book and Special Collections Division and in the Law Library contains important early printed works, including the 1494 Basel edition of Columbus's 1493 letter of discovery and extremely rare imprints of Spanish legal interest, such as, *Leyes del quaderno nuevo de las rentas delas alcavalas* (Burgos, 1491), *Leyes del Estilo* (Burgos, 1498), and *Repertorium de pravitate haereticorum* (Valencia, 1494). The Library recently acquired another rare example of fifteenth-century printing, a work commissioned by King John II of Portugal, Vasco Fernandes de Lucena's *Velasci Ferdinandi utriusique iuris consulti . . . ad Innocentium, viii. pontificem maximum de obedientia Oratio* (Rome, 1488). That early account of Portuguese explorations and discoveries was presented to Pope Innocent VIII, thus informing the pontiff of the commencement of the

OPPOSITE. *T-O Map. In Saint Isidorus [Bishop of Seville]. Etymologiarum sive originum libri XX. Augsburg, Gunther Zainer, 1472.* The T-O map shown here represents one of the earliest examples of medieval *mappae mundi*. Originally drawn between 622 and 633 as an illustration for Isidore's *Etymologiarum. . . .* , the most famous of his thirty encyclopedias and historical works, this map has the distinction of being the first printed world map, appearing in 1472 in an incunabula volume housed in the Rare Book and Special Collections Division. Dividing the world into the three known continents (Europe, Africa, Asia), this scheme used the T to represent, horizontally, the Don and the Nile (or possibly the Red Sea), the traditional separation of Europe and Africa from Asia, and, vertically, the Mediterranean Sea, giving the easterly orientation. The T also represented the tau cross, a mystical Christian symbol placing Jerusalem, their center of the world, at the intersection of the horizontal and vertical section. The O encircling the T portrayed the common ancient and medieval idea of a world surrounded by water. In the transitional period before Columbus's first voyage, it was not unusual to find all types of *mappae mundi* coexisting with the more realistic and practical portolan chart and the scientific work of Ptolemy. *(Vollbehr Collection, Rare Book and Special Collections Division)*

OPPOSITE. *Contador maior i texzorero. In Felipe Guamám Poma de Ayala. Nueva corónica y buen gobierno [facsimile of early seventeenth-century manuscript]. Paris, 1936.* To keep an account of the numbers of men, cattle, and goods, the Inca of the Andean region employed *quipucamayoc,* experts who used a decimal system to collect data of interest to the state; the data were maintained on stringed devices called quipus. Guamán Poma de Ayala illustrates such a civil servant. Each expert passed on his information to his superior, who in turn did the same, until finally all the information came together in Cuzco. Poma de Ayala, a chronicler of the Inca, was a descendant of Túpac Inca Yupanqui, one of the Inca rulers. His manuscript, which was not uncovered until 1908 and only reproduced in a limited edition in 1936, was completed in 1587, when it was presented to the King of Spain. The work provides valuable ethnographic and social information about the Incan society and its relations, after conquest, with the Spanish administration. *(General Books Collection)*

European age of discovery. As the Library's 100,000,001st item, that invaluable treasure, in the Rare Book and Special Collections Division, was acquired through a gift from Madison Council member John E. Velde, Jr.

For more than eight centuries, Sephardic Jews have spoken and written Spanish, even following their 1492 expulsion from Spain. The written form of their Ladino language uses Hebrew characters. One of the many interesting Luso-Hispanic collections in the library is a group of some six hundred Ladino volumes in the Hebraic Section of the African and Middle Eastern Division. Henry V. Besso's bibliography, *Ladino Books in the Library of Congress* (1963), lists nearly three hundred titles, the earliest of which is eleventh-century Bahya Ben Joseph Ibn Pakuda's *Sefer Jovot ha-Levavot (El dover de los corasones),* printed in Constantinople in 1550.

The concordances of texts by eleventh-century Spanish King Alfonso X from libraries in Paris, El Escorial, Madrid, the Vatican, and the British Library are found on 112 microfiches in the Microform Reading Room. That collection contains an early history of Spain, and works on astrology, games, and other topics. The Rare Book and Special Collections Division's copy of Isidore of Seville's *Etymologiarum sive originum libri XX* (1472) contains the first printed map, the seventh-century Spanish bishop's famous T-O world map.

The *Archivo Biográfico de España, Portugal e Iberoamérica,* also in the Library's Microform Reading Room, provides some two hundred thousand biographical entries on well-known Hispanic and Portuguese figures from the Roman period to the beginning of the twentieth century. The collection, on 1,143 microfiches, was compiled from 700 volumes of biographical references published between the seventeenth and the twentieth centuries. That rich biographical source is complemented by Alberto and Arturo García Carraffa's eighty-eight-folio *Enciclopedia heráldica-genealógica de apellidos españoles y americanos* (1919–1963) in the Library's general books collection. The *Family History Library,* a 2,020-microfiche catalog (now also on CD-ROM in the Local History and Genealogy Reading Room), identifies the thousands of reels of microfilm of governmental and church records from the sixteenth to the twentieth centuries on the Luso-Hispanic world located in the Family History Library of the Church of Jesus Christ of Latter-Day Saints in Salt Lake City, Utah.

Roman, customary, and Visigothic law, the influence of the Moors, and *fueros* provide the strands from which the legal mosaic of Spain and Portugal has been woven, and the Law Library holds noteworthy examples among its 1,500 rare book volumes. The thirteenth- century manuscript *Fuero Juzgo,* on vellum, is the Library of Congress's earliest work on Visigothic law. The Library also houses the milestones of the Spanish legal process, including the circa 1265 *Siete Partidas* (in a rare 1491 Seville printing), the 1310 *Leyes de Estiló* (in 1502 and 1540 Salamanca printings), the *Ordenanças reales de Castilla* (in 1566 and 1574 Salamanca editions), the 1505 *Leyes de Toro* (in a 1531 printing and 1527 and 1544 glosses), *Fuero Real* (in a 1501 Saragossa printing), and the official *Recopilación de las leyes destos reynos hechos por mandado de la magestad catholica del Rey don Philippe segundo* (in the first edition of 1567, and in 1571, 1581, 1640, and 1723 editions). All of these works are complemented by complete holdings of significant legal analyses. The *Law of the Indies*, which codified royal orders for Spain's colonies, issued by Castile and Aragón, begins the Library's comprehensive holdings of Spanish colonial legislation.

Along with comprehensive coverage of legislation existing at the national level, the Law Library holdings include the official gazettes of different regions and the *fueros* of Cataluña, País Vasco, Galicia, Aragón, Las Canarias, País Valenciano, Andalucia, Baleares, Extremadura, Castilla y Léon, Murcia, and Castilla La Mancha. Also found are modern civil, penal, criminal, and commercial codes which began to appear in Spain after 1880. That collection supports broad study of legislation, court reports, general works, legal education, jurisprudence and philosophy of law, legal history, civil law, commercial law, civil procedure, criminal law, constitutional law, administrative law, and labor legislation.

This collection contains historical landmarks of Portuguese jurisprudence, an excellent collection of colonial legislation, and comprehensive holdings of contemporary legislation issued at the national level. Within the Law Library collection are examples of such legal monuments as the Treaty of Tordesillas (1494) through which Spain and Portugal divided the non-Christian world. Present, too, are laws passed by Philip II of Spain in his role as Philip I of Portugal during the Spanish captivity (1580 to 1640). Royal decrees are here accompanied by all of the country's constitutions. These include the liberal constitution of 1822 and the Salazar-influenced constitution of 1933.

For Portuguese colonial legislation, the Law Library has the *Political, Civil and Criminal Statute of the Natives of Guinea, Angola and Mozambique* (1929) and the revised *Statute of the Portuguese Natives of the Provinces of Guinea, Angola and Mozambique* (1954).

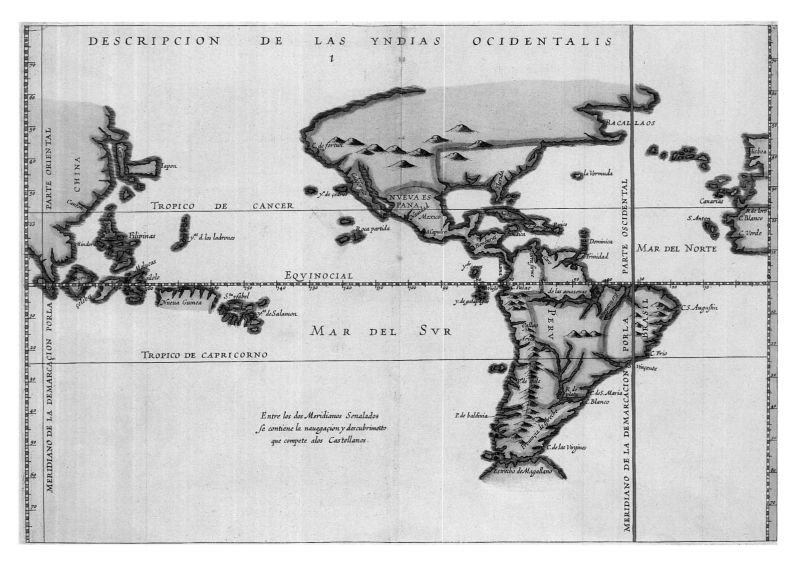

Entre los dos Meridianos Senalados
se contiene la nauegaçion y descubrimeito
que compete alos Castellanos.

Descripción de las Yndias Ocidentalis [printed map]. In Antonio de Herrera y Tordesillas. Description des Indes Occidentales. Amsterdam: M. Colin, 1622. This map describes the extent of Spanish possessions in America. The 1494 lines of demarcation, agreed upon by Spain and Portugal as a result of the Treaty of Tordesillas, divide America from Europe on the east and from Asia on the west. This map was part of the multivolume historical work by Herrera, Spain's official historian, *Historia general de los hechos de los castellanos en las islas y tierra firme del mar océano (1601–1615).* The work relates events of discovery, pacification, and settlement by Spaniards in America between 1492 and 1555. He availed himself of all the documents in the possession of the crown and the Council of the Indies, using them so extensively that for almost two centuries his work constituted an easy means of access to numerous unpublished documents and manuscripts. Copies of the *Historia general* are located in the Library's Rare Book and Special Collections Division. *(Vault Map Collection, Geography and Map Division)*

Among its holdings of labor legislation are the *Regulations on Native Labour* (1911) and *General Regulations on Native Labour in the Portuguese Colonies* (1914). In the collection with the official gazette are the *Boletin Geral das Colónias* and the *Boletin Geral do Ultramar* and primary sources encompassing Portuguese legal publications issued during the twentieth century colonial period including the *Nova Legislação Ultramarina* (1953–1969), *Legislação mandada aplicar ao Ultramar Português* (1926–1963, 1965–1966), and *Legislação Portuguesa* (1909–1931).

For the study of the Spanish Civil War (1936–1939), the Motion Picture, Broadcasting, and Recorded Sound Division has a collection of 16-mm prints of newsreels and documentaries, constituting part of an extensive collection of German films, produced from 1933 to 1945. Among documentaries held about the Spanish Civil War are *Alkazar* (German-language version, 1939), *Bethune* (Canada, 1964), *Between the Wars, no. 12: The Spanish Civil War* (U.S., 1978), *Los Canadienses* (Canada, 1976), *Deutsche Freiwillige in Spanien* (Germany, 1939), *The Good Fight* (U.S., 1984), *Heart of Spain* (U.S., 1937), *Helden in Spanien* (Germany, 1938), *Im Kampf gegen den Weltfeind* (Germany, 1939), *Madrid: Tumba del Fascio: Segunda Jornada* (Spain, 1936), *Sierra de Teruel* (France/Spain, 1938), *The Spanish Civil War, Granada TV* (England, 1983), *The Spanish Earth* (U.S., 1937), and *The Twentieth Century: War in Spain, CBS-TV* (U.S., 1960). The Manuscript Division has papers of the pool of British insurance companies involved in providing coverage for businesses in civil war-torn Spain and copies of the minutes of the *Junta de defensa de Madrid* of General José Miaja Menant, the Republic's commander in the 1936 defense of Madrid, who coined the term "fifth column." The Microform Reading Room's holdings of the Gibbs Archives consists of the nineteenth- and twentieth-century business records of a British firm with substantial interests in Spain. A collection of related materials is found in the GARY YANKER POSTER COLLECTION and in Lot 3929 in the photographic collection of the Prints and Photographs Division, as well as in books and periodicals in the general books collections of the Library of Congress.

The SPANISH CIVIL WAR: FO 849, FOREIGN OFFICE, INTERNATIONAL COMMITTEE FOR THE APPLICATION OF THE AGREEMENT REGARDING NON-INTERVENTION IN SPAIN 1936–1939 COLLECTION (twenty-four reels of microfilm) is in the Microform Reading Room. It contains the British Foreign Office's File 849 comprising the stenographic notes of the meetings of the International Committee for the Application of the Agreement Regarding Non-Intervention in Spain, the International Board for Non-Intervention memoranda (March 1937-March 1939), and other bodies formed to deal with intervention at the time of the Spanish Civil War.

Bardasano, José. 1936 18 de Julio 1937. Color lithograph poster, 1937. The bitter conflict between republican and nationalist forces during the first year of Spain's Civil War (1936–1939) is reflected in this poster. It marked the first anniversary of the date on which nationalist leader General Francisco Franco launched his military campaign against the Spanish Republic. The poster appeals to the indignation of the republican side toward foreign and foreign-backed aggressors. It had been hoped that within the year the Franco-led nationalists would be defeated. *(Poster Collection, Prints and Photographs Division)*

OPPOSITE. *Hernando Cortés and the Spanish Soldiers Confront the Indians. In Fray Diego Durán.* La Historia antigua de la Nueva España. *1585 [Manuscript facsimile, ca. nineteenth century].* The fierce confrontation between the Spaniards under Cortés and the followers of Moctezuma received full treatment in Father's Durán's manuscript illustrated history of Mexico, compiled shortly after the early sixteenth-century conquest. The Mexica (Aztec) peoples confronted a powerful Spanish force supplemented by a sizable number of allies from the area surrounding Tenochtitlán (later named Mexico City) during the 1519–1521 campaigns. Durán's informants have skillfully distinguished Indian peoples from the European invaders, with a ghostly white image representing the Spanish. The Library of Congress acquired this extremely rare facsimile manuscript in the Peter Force Collection purchase in 1867. *(Peter Force Collection, Manuscript Division)*

In October 1492 Christopher Columbus and his crew reached the Bahamas. From that time forward Europeans and the people living in the continents of the Western Hemisphere now known to us as the Americas, North and South, came into permanent contact. That encounter took numerous forms, generating responses from various sides. These reactions depended as much on the circumstances and world view of indigenous groups as they did on European objectives and values.

The interactions among groups have produced complex relationships. Varying forms of resistance and adaptation among Indian, African, Asian, and European peoples occurred throughout the region, and that process of evolution in the Americas is strongly reflected in the Library of Congress collections.

The Manuscript Division possesses an extensive body of photoreproduced documents from foreign archives acquired through special copying programs during the twentieth century. Both colonial and independence period materials for the Americas, including materials from Spain's Real Academia de la Historia, Archivo Histórico General, Biblioteca del Palacio, Biblioteca Nacional, Archivo General de Indias, Biblioteca Colombina, Archivo General de Simancas, Biblioteca Pública (Toledo) and the national archives of Argentina, Chile, Cuba, Puerto Rico, Venezuela, the Vatican (Peruvian dispatches, 1603–1875), Great Britain (British Foreign Office Papers on Panama, 1827–1919), France, and several Mexican archives, including the Archivo General de la Nación, Archivo de la Secretaría de Relaciones Exteriores, Biblioteca Nacional, Biblioteca Benjamín Franklin, Archivo General de Mérida, the Archive of the Bishop of Mérida, the Museo Nacional de Arqueología, Historia y Etnografía, and the Banco de México are found there. Photocopied records on the Luso-Hispanic world from these same archives are found in the collections of the Geography and Map, Rare Book and Special Collections, and the Prints and Photographs Divisions.

Invaluable as source materials, these copied documents provide primary information on the Americas from the Spanish colonial administration in Chile, Charcas, Mexico, Guatemala, Philippines, Nueva Granada, Santo Domingo, Cuba, and Spanish administrative locations in what is now the United States. Among these documents are found official correspondence, local reports, maps, cryptic messages, literary tracts, and censuses. While these substantial and invaluable materials for the most part provide coverage for Spanish administration in the United States, both in its southeastern and southwestern regions, additional rolls of microfilm contain documents on Mexico. The publication *The Hispanic World 1492–1898; El mundo hispánico 1492–1898* (1994) guides one into the treasures in the Spanish archival portion of this copied collection in the Manuscript, Geography and

Map, Prints and Photographs, and Rare Book and Special Collections Divisions.

In the Rare Book and Special Collections Division are some four hundred early publications printed in Spanish American colonies, 1544–1820. This SPAN-ISH AMERICAN IMPRINTS COLLECTION contains original works primarily from Mexico, Peru, and Guatemala, although imprints from other areas appear. These works include some of the earliest publications printed in the Western Hemisphere. One can find in the collection Indian language grammars and vocabularies, general histories, religious publications, statutes of the Inquisition, and juridical and political writings. Among the collection's treasures are a 1544 copy of Bishop Juan de Zumárraga's *Doctrina Breve* and original editions by Horacio Carochi, Pablo José de Arriaga, Maturino Gilberti, Luís Lopez Juan Bautista, Juan de Grijalva, Alonso de Molina, Bishop Juan de Palafox y Mendoza, Pedro de Peralta Barnuevo Rocha y Benavides, and Carlos de Sigüenza y Góngora. In the Law Library is

First page. Epistola de insulis nuper inventis [printed letter] [Christopher Columbus]. Rome, Stephan Plannck, 1493. This book contains the first printed European descriptions of the people and places in America. While homeward bound in mid-February 1493, Columbus wrote a brief report concerning his discoveries. He depicts the inhabitants, whom he calls Indians, as kind and timid, willing to do much for little, and ready to convert to Christianity. Within six weeks of his arrival in Europe, a Latin edition of Columbus's letter was printed in Rome by Stephan Plannck. It was this Latin letter that spread the news of discovery throughout Europe. The Library's copy of the Latin edition is the foundation stone of its vast Americana collection. *(Incunable Collection, Rare Book and Special Collections Division)*

found the 1563 Mexican *Cedulario de Puga*, the first law book printed in the Americas. The Music Division has the 1576 Mexican imprint by Pedro Ocharte, of the *graduale dominicale*, the Library's earliest printed American book of music.

The LATIN AMERICAN IMPRINTS BEFORE 1800 COLLECTION, selected from the bibliographical surveys of the Chilean bibliophile José Toribio Medina, is available in the Microform Reading Room on 248 reels of microfilm. Among the themes represented are those on politics, religion, literature and education as well as histories, *relaciones*, descriptive and practical works, and a variety of government publications.

The library of Peter Force, a collection of more than 65,000 manuscripts, books, newspapers, and maps on American history, early American imprints, and incunabula, was purchased by act of Congress in 1867. In the course of preparing his *Documentary History of the American Revolution*, this Washington publisher and politician (1790–1868) assembled what was probably the largest private collection in the United States of printed and manuscript sources on American history. Among the items is a twenty-five-volume Hispanic collection, consisting primarily of manuscript copies of works about the Americas by various Spanish writers, including Bartolomé de las Casas. Items of particular value and use are Fray Diego Durán's *Historia Antigua de la Nueva España* (1585) which is a history of the native peoples of Mexico's Central Valley, a record of their calendar, and other activities; Fray Jerónimo de Alcalá's history of the Tarascan peoples of western Mexico, *Relación de . . . Mechuacan* (1537–41); and Mariano Fernández de Echevarría y Veitia's sixteenth-century *Historia del origen de las gentes . . .* which includes copies of seven Mexica calendars.

The Rare Book and Special Collections Division houses 5,193 books and manuscripts, containing incunabula and early Americana, donated by John Boyd Thacher (1847–1909), a New York manufacturer and politician. Thacher drew upon this extensive collection for his publications *The Continent of America* (1896) and *Christopher Columbus* (1903–1904). It is highlighted by copies of thirty-four early editions of Ptolemy's *Geographia*, an illustrated 1494 Basel edition of Columbus's 1493 letter on America, three pre-1510 editions of Martin Waldseemüller's *Cosmographiae Introductio* in which the name America first appears, and the unique 1503 Angelo Trevisan manuscript on Spanish explorations in America (1492–1500) and Portuguese voyages to Brazil and India (1497–1502).

The Library of Congress has all the major histories of America which describe Spanish and Portuguese conquest and colonization. These range from contemporaries of the early European Age of Discovery such as Pietro Martire d'Anghiera and Gonzalo Fernández de Oviedo to those by travelers in Spanish

America in the early colonial period such as Girolamo Benzoni, whose *Historia del Mondo Nuovo* is present in Italian (1572), French (1579), Latin (1578), German (late sixteenth century), and Dutch (1610) editions.

There are very many first editions despite their great rarity. The earliest of histories of the Americas, *De Orbe Novo*, by Pietro Martire de Anghiera is found in its stages of presentation, in 1511, 1524, and 1553 editions. An English translation of the work by Richard Eden, *The Decades of the Newe Worlde or West India* (1555), and the 1577 reissue by Richard Willis, *The historie of travayle into the West and east Indies*, are located in the Rare Book and Special Collections Division. The Library of Congress holds Gonzalo Fernández de Oviedo's (1478–1557) 1526 edition of his *Natural hystoria delas Indias*, the 1535 edition of his *Historia general de las Indias*, and his 1547 *Corónica de las Indias*.

Works on the Spanish conquests in America including Francisco López de Gómara's 1553 *Historia general de las Indias* on Mexico, or Bartolomé de las Casas's *Brevissima relación de la destrucción de las Indias* (1552) on the Caribbean world, or works by José de Acosta, Francisco de Xerez, Pedro Cieza de León, Agustín de Zárate, and Garcilaso de la Vega on Peru, or by André Thevet and Jean de Léry on Brazil, or by Ulrich Schmidel and Theodor de Bry on Rio de la Plata, or by Nuñez Cabeza de Vaca and Garcilaso de la Vega on Florida and Texas are all found in the Rare Book and Special Collections Division.

The HENRY HARRISSE COLLECTION, in the Library's Rare Book and Special Collections and the Geography and Map Divisions, contains publications, papers, and maps on early American exploration. Perhaps best known for *Bibliotheca Americana Vetutissima*, a description of over three hundred writings on America published between 1492 and 1551, Harrisse (1829–1910) wrote extensively on Christopher and Ferdinand Columbus, John and Sebastian Cabot, and the early voyages of American exploration.

Through his 1915 bequest, the Library of Congress acquired his personal collection which is in the Rare Book and Special Collections Division. In addition to more than two hundred volumes, the collection preserves correspondence pertaining to Harrisse's research, an original letter by Pietro Martire d'Anghiera, and a circa 1553 manuscript description of a voyage along the northern coast of South America. Among the fourteen rare manuscript maps and one view from the Harrisse bequest in the Geography and Map Division are maps of North and South America, including ones of Habana harbor, Cuba, Hispaniola, and the Bahamas (1639) by Joan Vingboons, cartographer of the Prince of Nassau. Harrisse's study collection of 600 photographs, facsimiles, and tracings of early maps is also in that Division.

The naming of America. In Martin Waldseemüller. Cosmographiae introductio. St. Dié, 1507. This extremely rare work contains the first suggestion that the area of Columbus's discovery be named "America" in honor of Amerigo Vespucci, who recognized that a "New World," the so-called fourth part of the world, had been reached through Columbus's voyage. Before that time, there was no name that collectively identified the Western Hemisphere. The earlier Spanish explorers referred to the area as the Indies believing, as did Columbus, that it was a part of eastern Asia. *(Thacher Collection, Rare Book and Special Collections Division)*

Balsa boat on Lake Titicaca. Black and white photograph. [ca. 1940]. The form of transportation depicted in this ca. 1940 photograph is time honored in the highlands of Peru and Bolivia. Images of the balsa, or reed boats of Lake Titicaca appeared in pre-Inca poetry of the Mochica culture of the Andean region. *(General Geographical Collection, Prints and Photographs Division)*

Columbus's Book of Privileges in the Manuscript Division is a 1502 manuscript on vellum of the various hereditary grants, charters, and privileges made to Columbus by Fernando and Isabel and the Papal Bulls issued by Alexander VI in May and October 1493. One of the Library's most valuable treasures, the interest attached to this codex is heightened by the fact that it was compiled by public notaries under the personal direction of Columbus shortly before he embarked on his fourth and final voyage to America. The Library's example of the *Book of Privileges* is one of only three vellum originals; the other originals are located in Genoa and Paris. In 1818 Edward Everett purchased in Florence the eighty-folio-page manuscript on vellum which the Library of Congress purchased from the family in 1897.

For the study of the earliest period in colonial Mexico and Peru, especially the activities of Hernando Cortés and Francisco Pizarro, the HARKNESS COLLECTION, in the Manuscript Division, is an invaluable resource. In 1928 and 1929 Edward Stephen Harkness (1874–1940), an American philanthropist, presented the collection of documents to the Library of Congress.

The 2,939-folio Mexican manuscripts segment relates primarily to the 1566 Cortés-Avila conspiracy to overthrow the government of New Spain and to the affairs of Hernando Cortés and his family between 1525 and 1565. Of particular interest are the confirmation of Cortés's coat of arms and the extremely rare 1531 Huexotzinco Codex, a tribute document on *amatl* paper, prepared by the indigenous peoples of Huexotzinco.

The character of the 1,405 folios of Peruvian manuscripts in the HARKNESS COLLECTION varies. A great part is composed of original notarial documents (1531–1618). Other documents include royal *cédulas* (1555–1610), viceregal decrees (1556–1651, 1740) and the minutes and acts of the town councils of Chachapoyas (1538–1545) and San Juan de la Frontera de Guamanga (1539–1547). Forty-eight documents relate to the families of Francisco Pizarro and Diego de Almagro, key figures in the Spanish conquest of Peru. Two undated and anonymous sixteenth-century manuscript charts on vellum of the west coast of South and Central America are in the VELLUM CHART COLLECTION in the Geography and Map Division.

A second major body of 162 manuscripts relating to the history of Spanish America during its colonial period was donated by Hans P. Kraus in 1969. Located in the Manuscript Division, this collection is known as the HANS P. KRAUS COLLECTION OF HISPANIC AMERICAN MANUSCRIPTS. Focusing on colonial Mexico, the KRAUS COLLECTION contains documents on exploration, government, the Inquisition, economic conditions, Indian relations, and the impending loss of land to

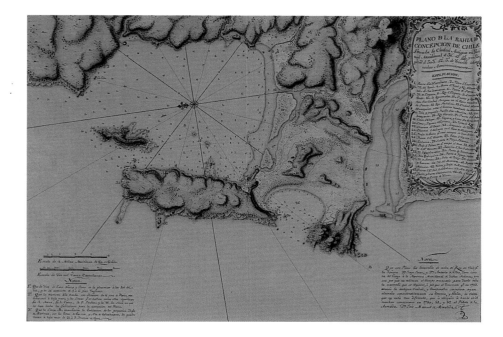

[Portion]. Plano de la Bahía de Concepción de Chile . . . 1782. Jorge Juan and Antonio de Ulloa. Real Escuela de Navegación, Cádiz. This plan was prepared in 1744 (later copied) by Jorge Juan and Antonio de Ulloa who were commissioned by the Spanish crown to report on Peru and Ecuador in the 1730s. They delivered scathing indictments of the abuses of colonial rulers and the treatment of Indians in field and factory, and helped to provoke the belated reforms of Charles III. The cartographic endeavors of the Real Escuela de Navegación, Cádiz, and the Spanish navy in general in the eighteenth century are represented in a unique collection of nearly 400 manuscript charts and plans bearing various dates from 1712 to 1848 in the Geography and Map Division. Early charts of the Falkland/Malvinas (1770) and the detailed studies of directions and soundings in harbors and coastal regions throughout Latin America, in addition to the maps resulting from the eighteenth-century scientific expedition of Jorge Juan and Antonio de Ulloa are some of the collection's highlights. *(Maggs Map Collection, Geography and Map Division)*

Anglo-American settlers in Florida. From the archives of Juan de Zumárraga, first bishop of Mexico, there are papers dating from 1527 to 1660 that include the signatures of Emperor Charles V, Isabella of Portugal, Philip II, Juana, and Cardinal García de Loaysa. Other documents pertain to the civil administration in the sixteenth-century Spanish Indies which throw light on the drafting of the New Laws of 1542 and the career of Bartolomé de las Casas. The KRAUS COLLECTION includes documents on the viceregal administration, the history of Spanish Florida, Hernando Alvarado Tezozomoc's chronicle on the history of the Aztec peoples, and on explorations and other activities of Amerigo Vespucci, Giovanni da Verrazzano, Alvar Núñez Cabeza de Vaca, Pedro de Ursúa, and Lope de Aguirre. The HENRY A. MONDAY COLLECTION of Mexican manuscripts and documents (1522–1935) in the Manuscript Division concerns primarily the activities of the Dominican Order in Puebla and Catholic Church documents for colonial Mexico.

The Library's Geography and Map Division has an extremely rich collection of original, printed, and photoreproduced maps of Hispanic and Portuguese America. Among many items in this truly outstanding collection is a copy of Juan de la Cruz Cano y Olmedilla's 1775 official map of South America, other detailed cartographic items for America, a host of individual maps and charts such as those by Francisco Matías Celi, Tomás López, and Juan Enrique de la Rigada, and one of only two extant copies of Diego Gutiérrez's extraordinary 1562 printed map of America, which was given to the Library by Lessing J. Rosenwald. That last map, the largest printed map of America at the time, provides detailed coastal

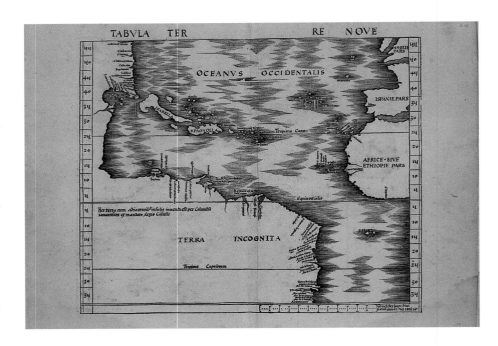

Map of America. Martin Waldseemüller. [Ptolemaeus] Geographiae Opus Novissima Traductione . . . Strasbourg, 1513. The first appearance of a map of America in a Ptolemy atlas occurred in the 1513 Strasbourg edition, which included a series of new maps, based on findings from recent European explorations. Martin Waldseemüller of St. Dié began work on this new edition of Ptolemy about 1505 and compiled the maps. In this work, America remains as "Terra Incognita" and Columbus is credited with informing Isabel and Fernando of its existence. *(Geography and Map Division)*

and interior information of the Western Hemisphere. Another rich manuscript map collection, the MAGGS COLLECTION, from the Royal School for Navigation (Cádiz), contains about four hundred eighteenth- and early nineteenth-century coastal charts of the Americas, from the Gulf of Mexico to Tierra del Fuego.

The numerous Spanish, Portuguese, Dutch, French, and British cartographic objects and printed and manuscript maps and atlases of Luso-Hispanic America are too numerous to specify. A prime collection of reproductions of Spanish maps of America is the Duke of Alba's *Mapas españoles de América* (Madrid, 1951), and an important adjunct is the Spanish Servicio Histórico Militar's publication *Cartografía de Ultramar* (1955–1968), based on the irreplaceable contents of the archives in the Spanish Ministerio de Guerra.

The JOHANN GEORG KOHL COLLECTION, containing early American maps and papers compiled by the German geographer Kohl, is found in the Geography and Map and the Manuscript Divisions. When Kohl (1808–1878) came to the United States in 1854, he brought his collection of facsimiles of maps on the discovery and exploration of the Americas copied through years of research in European libraries and archives. Kohl's drawings represented the most comprehensive collection of cartographic reproductions existing in America at that time. In 1856 the U.S. Congress commissioned Kohl to duplicate his drawings for a proposed catalog of early maps of America, and in 1903 they were transferred to the Library of Congress. A catalog, compiled by Justin Winsor in 1886 and

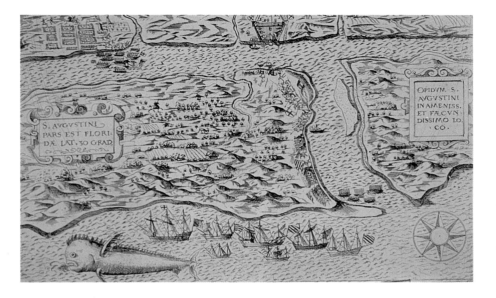

reprinted with an index in 1904, describes 474 Kohl facsimiles in the Geography and Map Division.

For further study of Spain's early contacts in America, the Microform Reading Room has on microfilm the forty-two-volume *Colección de documentos inéditos relativos al descubrimiento, conquista y organización de las antiguas posesiones españoles de América y Oceania* (1864–1884) and the twenty-five-volume *Colección de documentos inéditos relativos al descubrimiento, conquista y organización de las antiguas posesiones españolas de ultramar* (1885–1932) contain unpublished thirteenth- to eighteenth-century Spanish archival documents including papers relating to Cuba, the Philippines and Mexico and the papers of the Council of the Indies.

Hans P. Kraus, in the 1970s, donated to the Library of Congress a rich collection of documents, manuscripts, maps, and books related to the activities of Francis Drake in America and Europe in the late sixteenth century. One of the earliest maps of St. Augustine, Florida, items related to Drake's raids on Spanish America and Spain in the sixteenth century, and accounts of early travel through the Straits of Magellan are included in that collection.

Conflict among European powers in Hispanic and Portuguese America is fully documented in the Library's collections. In the Manuscript Division are found the Dutch West Indian Company materials 1568–1695; the Alice Bache Gould Puerto Rican memorial collection containing eighteenth- and nineteenth-century materials on Puerto Rican politics, religion, and education; the Vernon-Wager papers

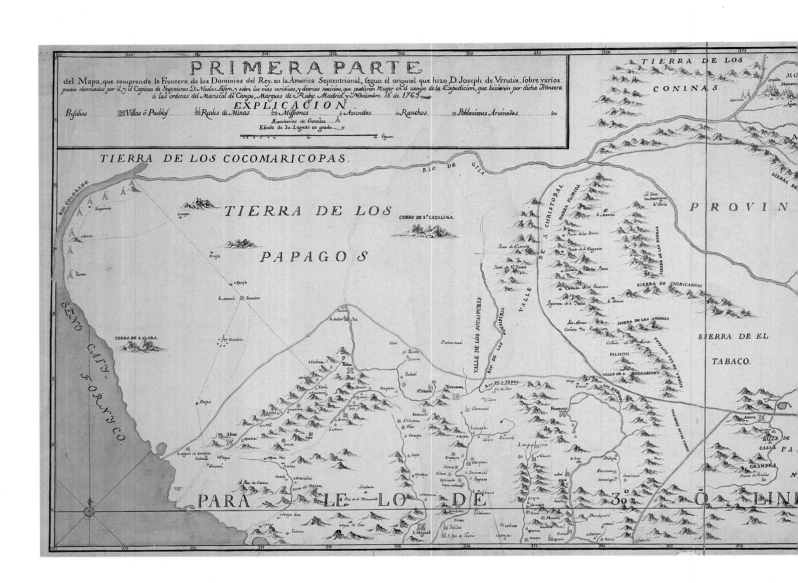

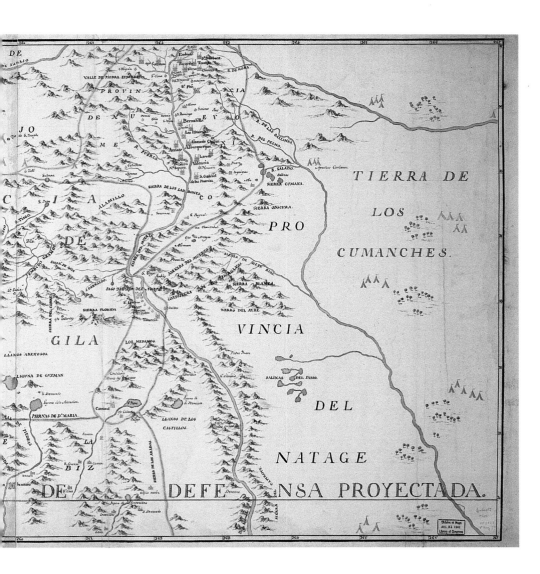

[Map of New Mexico, Arizona, Texas, 1766–1768]. *Josef Urrutia and Nicolás La Fora. México, 1771. Manuscript map, 1 sheet of 4.* During 1766–68, on the instruction of Charles III of Spain, the Marqués de Rubí inspected the presidios on the northern frontier of New Spain, from the Gulf of California to Louisiana, in order to recommend measures for improving the presidio system. He was accompanied by Nicolás de La Fora and Josef Urrutia, of the Royal Engineers, who prepared a map and report of the tour that provided much information on the Indian peoples and conditions along the frontier. In 1772, the king issued a regulation based on the recommendations made as a result of the expedition, prescribing the manner of conducting relations with the Indians, the duties of the commandant inspector and other military personnel, and providing for a cordon of fifteen presidios, at intervals of about forty leagues, from Sonora to Texas. The object was to prevent Apache raids from the north into settled areas and to bring the Indians under military control. The Library of Congress has a copy of the four-sheet map of the expedition; the British Library has the diary of La Fora and the individual presidio plans. *(Vault Map Collection, Geography and Map Division)*

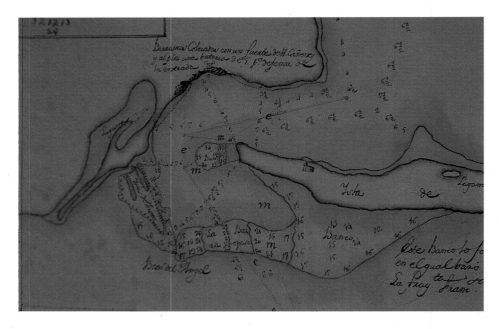

[Portion]. Plano de la bahía de Pansacola [sic].
Antonio Donato Paredes. 1782. Manuscript map.
Prepared shortly after the recapture of
Pensacola from the British by the Spanish
during the U.S. Revolutionary War, this
detailed chart provides accurate information on the entrance and locations of forts,
churches, and Campbelltown in Pensacola
Bay. The successful 1781 Spanish offensive
under Bernardo de Gálvez, on Pensacola,
effectively removed the British threat on
the western flank of the American revolutionaries. Invaluable original cartographic
and other documentary records of Spain's
presence in what became the United
States are found throughout the Library
of Congress's rich collections. *(Vault Map
Collection, Geography and Map Division)*

containing correspondence of two British admirals pertaining to pirates and naval
operations in the Caribbean during the War of Jenkins Ear; and the Irene Wright
collection of transcripts of Spanish American documents from the Archivo General de Indias. In addition, one can find there the George Chalmers collection of
correspondence and administrative commercial documents pertaining to the British
West Indies (1670–1825) with some materials on other areas of the Caribbean, Honduras, Brazil, and West Florida; and British Admiral George Cockburn's logbooks
on 1788–1812 Spanish American revolutionary activities. The 1777 boundary dispute in South America between Spain and Portugal is the subject of a collection in
the Geography and Map Division of the boundary commission's maps prepared by
Francisco Requena; also found there is the 1782 map of the Peruvian royalist forces'
troop movements against Tupac Amaru II.

In considering the long-term Luso-Hispanic presence in the United States,
under Spain until 1821 and under Mexico until 1848, numerous collections are
available for fruitful study. In the Manuscript Division, the JEANNETTE THURBER
CONNOR COLLECTION of transcripts of sixteenth- to nineteenth-century Spanish archival documents on Spanish Florida; the WOODBURY LOWERY COLLECTION
of transcripts relating to the Spanish presence in the Southeastern United States

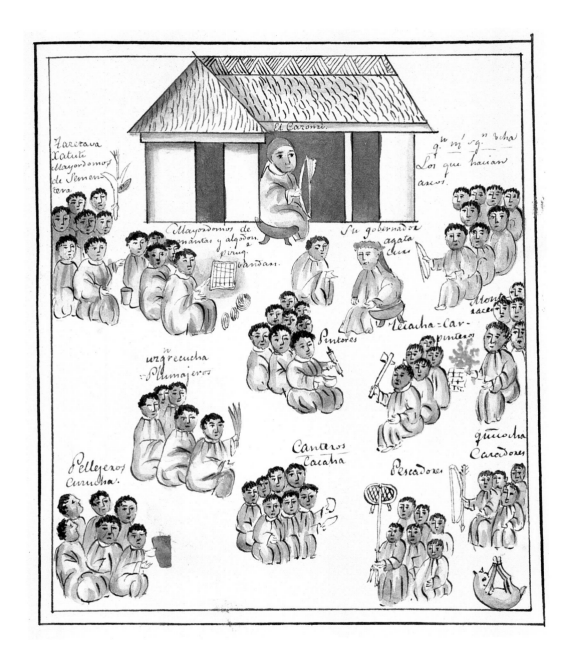

Occupational groups. Ink and wash drawing. In Relación de las ceremonias y ritos y población y gobierno de los indios de la provincia de Mechuacan, compiled by Fray Jeronimo de Alcalá. nineteenth-century manuscript copy of original, ca. 1540. The Relación is a well-illustrated manuscript from Mexico that chronicles the history and customs of the Tarascan people before as well as during the Spanish conquest in the area of Michoacán, Mexico. This copy, one of two in the United States, is a fine nineteenth-century manuscript facsimile of the original housed in the library of El Escorial in Spain. Although the work was written by a Franciscan friar, it is based largely on the accounts of informants among the Tarascan nobility and priests and thus is significant as a source from the Conquest period that essentially expresses an indigenous point of view. In the illustration, the artist depicted various occupational groups existing before the arrival of the Spanish. Groups of seated figures are placed with an object or symbol such as a net, a loom, a bow and an arrow, a writing instrument, feathers, etc., that identifies the occupation of a specific group. Figures in the upper portion of the illustration sit alone and are identified as being the *Cazonci* (or ruler) and his governor. *(Peter Force Collection, Manuscript Division)*

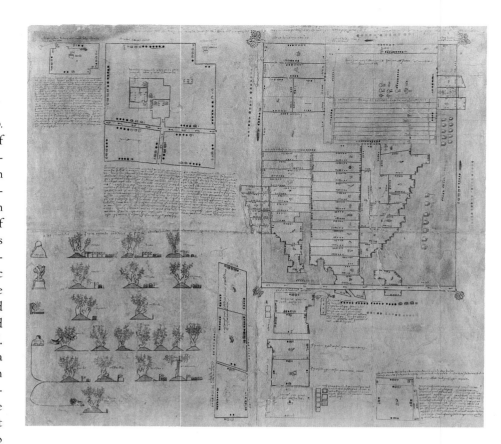

Oztoticpac Lands Map. Amate paper, ca. 1540. Mexico. Picture writing on manuscripts of amate paper or on animal skin is of unknown antiquity in Mesoamerica, although it substantially predates the arrival of Europeans to America. Following the Spanish conquest of Mexico in the first quarter of the sixteenth century, painted manuscripts in various native artistic traditions continued to be produced. In civil and economic matters Indian peoples and Spaniards alike found that maps, tribute registers, and cadastral and census documents derived from native traditions met a common need. The Oztoticpac (Mexico) Lands Map is a central Mexican pictorial document with Spanish and Nahuatl writing showing litigation surrounding the Oztoticpac estate within the city of Texcoco. The document involves the land and property ownership of the ruler of Texcoco, Don Carlos Ometochtli Chichimecatecotl, who was executed during the early days of the Spanish conquest. Most of the drawings on the map are plans of fields with indigenous measurements and place glyphs. Near the upper left is the plan of several houses within a precinct. On the upper right is a map showing about seventy-five plots of land. Nahuatl and Spanish descriptions appear. In the lower left are depictions of tree grafts, showing European fruit tree branches grafted to indigenous tree trunks. This unique cartographic object is the earliest recorded lawsuit or conflict in horticultural literature anywhere in the world. (*Vault Map Collection, Geography and Map Division*)

1551–1893; the LUIS DE ONIS correspondence on the Adams-Onís Treaty (1810–1816); the VICENTE SEBASTIAN PINTADO manuscripts (correspondence, maps, reports), by the last surveyor general of Spanish West Florida (1803–1817); and the SPANISH GOVERNMENT OF EAST FLORIDA COLLECTION with some 65,000 administrative and military documents (1777–1821) are rich sources for study.

The WOODBURY LOWERY COLLECTION in the Geography and Map and Manuscript Divisions contains 300 original and facsimile maps and eighteen volumes of notes and transcripts from Washington patent lawyer and historian Woodbury Lowery (1853–1906). The collection relates to the study of the former Spanish possessions within the United States. The eighteen volumes of Lowery's notes and transcripts in the Manuscript Division pertain to the early history of Florida, the subject of Lowery's *The Spanish Settlements Within the Present Limits of the United States* (1905), and to New Mexico, California, Texas, and Louisiana.

The WEST FLORIDA PAPERS, in the Manuscript Division, concern the government of Spain there, especially during the crucial late eighteenth- and early nineteenth-century periods. These papers contain information on the British in West Florida (1762–1783) and the conspirators in the 1810 West Florida Revolution,

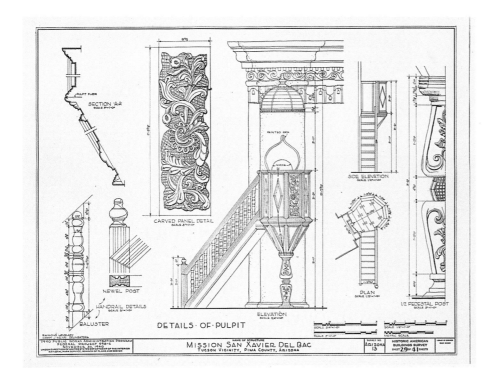

which separated the Louisiana portion of Spanish West Florida from Spain. Of utmost relevance to the West Florida papers are the correspondence and maps found in the Pintado documents previously noted. Pintado served as a surveyor in Louisiana from the late eighteenth century until 1805 and as surveyor general for all of Spanish West Florida from Pensacola during 1805 to 1817. Complementing all of these records are the PAPERS OF THE PANTON, LESLIE AND COMPANY, a twenty-six-reel microfilm collection in the Microform Reading Room, containing the records of a British firm in Spanish Pensacola which conducted trade throughout the region during the late eighteenth and the early nineteenth centuries.

The Microform Reading Room also has the DOCUMENTARY RELATIONS OF THE SOUTHWEST COLLECTION (on eighty-one microfiches) which includes indexes to primary documents on the southwestern part of what is now the United States from 1520 to 1820, with extensive lists of names of persons mentioned in the documents.

The long history of indigenous societies in the Americas is richly reflected in the general and special collections of the Library of Congress. Reproductions of

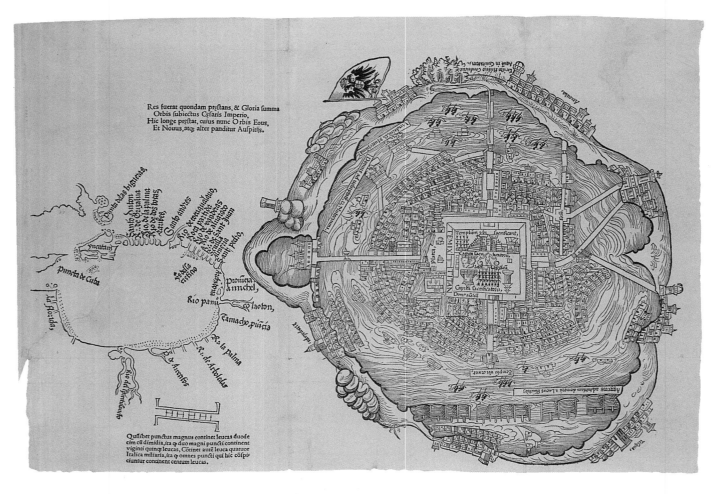

pre-Columbian and European-contact period Indian documents, including *codices*, are found in the Rare Book and Special Collections Division, in the general books collection, and in photographic copies in the Prints and Photographs Division's JOHN B. GLASS COLLECTION and the ARCHIVE OF HISPANIC CULTURE COLLECTION.

Numerous other records of Indian culture are found. A collection of original manuscripts and photocopies of Indian-language documents from Mesoamerica, from the sixteenth to the early twentieth century, is found in the WILLIAM GATES COLLECTION of historical and linguistic manuscripts in the Manuscript Division. A companion record in that same division, the 5,700-item RUDOLPH R. SCHULLER COLLECTION, acquired from Schuller in 1914, contains manuscript copies of archaeological, ethnographic, linguistic, and cartographic manuscripts of Central and South American areas. Over two hundred boxes and twenty-five volumes of dictionaries, vocabularies, translations of Mexica dramas, and other materials in the Indian languages of Mexico and Central America are located in miscellaneous collections in the Manuscript Division. A manuscript copy of Father José de Anchieta's *Arte de grammatica da lingoa mais usada na costa do brazil* (1595) is also found in the Manuscript Division.

The G.R.G. CONWAY COLLECTION contains copied documents on sixteenth-century Britons in Mexico from the *Inquisición* section of the *Archivo General y Público* in Mexico City and the *Archivo General de Indias* in Sevilla. That forty-five-volume set in the Manuscript Division is supported by papers on the Inquisition in New Mexico from the papers in the *Archivo General y Público* in Mexico City donated by France Scholes in 1930 and on the Inquisition in Texas from the same archive provided by Charles W. Hackett. In addition, some 3,500 typewritten pages of documents on the late eighteenth- and early nineteenth-century history of Spanish Texas was donated by Professor Hackett.

The HISTORIC AMERICAN BUILDINGS SURVEY, a collection of measured drawings, photographs, and data sheets documenting works of American architecture, in the Prints and Photographs Division, is the largest and most important architectural collection in that division. The project documented structures in all fifty states, Puerto Rico, the Virgin Islands, and the District of Columbia. Numerous buildings of the Hispanic period from the states of Alabama, Mississippi, Arizona, Louisiana, Florida, California, Colorado, New Mexico, Texas, and Puerto Rico are found in the records. Another source for reproductions of colonial period and pre-Columbian structures in Latin America is the ARCHIVE OF HISPANIC CULTURE COLLECTION, also in the Prints and Photographs Division.

The Microform Reading Room's *Archivo Franciscano*, on nineteen reels of microfilm (from the holdings of the Mexican *Instituto Nacional de Antropología e Historia*) contains sixteenth- to eighteenth-century documents from both Franciscan and non-Franciscan sources on that order's activities in Mexico, California, and the southwestern part of the United States. These documents address ecclesiastical, military, local history, missionary activity, Jesuit expulsion, exploration, discovery, conquest of new territories, and Indian relation topics.

Slavery tracts and pamphlets from the WEST INDIA COMMITTEE COLLECTION, at the Institute of Commonwealth Studies, are found on twenty-eight reels of microfilm in the Microform Reading Room. The collection consists mainly of early nineteenth-century publications from England and the West Indies, including works by Prime Minister George Canning, by the parliaments of Great Britain, Jamaica, the Bahamas, St. Vincent, and Barbados, by various Bible societies, and by noteworthy proponents and opponents of the continuation of slavery in the West Indies.

OPPOSITE. *Map of Mexico City and the Gulf of Mexico. In Hernando Cortés. Praeclara Ferdinandi Cortesii de Nova maris Hyspania narratio. [Norimbergae] [1524].* This map, actually two separate maps on one sheet, one of Tenochtitlán (Mexico City) prepared by the Mexicas and presented to Cortés as a gift in the 1519–1521 period, and a map of the Gulf Coast region of Mexico and the southeastern part of the present-day United States, was prepared either by the Mexica peoples or by a contemporary Spanish explorer. These maps appeared with the second letter of Hernando Cortés to Charles V, King of Spain. There is much in both of these maps to suggest that the drawings supplied to the Nuremberg engraver who prepared the printer's woodblock were based on Mexica (Aztec) originals. Cortés, anxious to inform and to impress Charles V, sent his lieutenant Juan de Ribera in 1522 to deliver samples of Aztec objets d'art and treasure to the royal court. Ribera also carried maps of Mexica origin which were examined by Peter Martyr. Martyr described one Aztec map that was thirty feet long painted on white cotton cloth, and a smaller native painting representing the town of Temistitan (Tenochtitlán) with its temples, bridges, and lakes. The volume in which the maps appear is part of the spectacular collection of illuminated imprints presented to the Library by Lessing J. Rosenwald. (Rosenwald Collection, Rare Book and Special Collections Division)

The development of the Library's Hispanic and Portuguese collections parallel the emergence of new republics in the Americas, as independence movements swept the Hemisphere throughout the nineteenth century. Materials for the study of the governments—presidencies, congresses, assemblies, courts of justice—of the region, such as records of congressional debates from their origin in the nineteenth century and official publications from republics and extensive research materials on related subjects, make the Library's holdings unequalled for completeness. The relationships of individuals and countries are reflected in the Library's manuscript, book, map, print, law, official publication, recording, and music collections.

The LUIS DOBLES SEGREDA COLLECTION, on microfilm, is a comprehensive record of publication from and about Costa Rica. The distinguished Costa Rican scholar and diplomat Dobles Segreda began his collection in 1910 in an effort to bring together as many writings as possible on his country, wherever published. The collection, purchased by the Library of Congress in 1943, contained more than 5,600 books and pamphlets issued between 1831 and the 1930s. The papers of Ephraim George Squier, in the Manuscript and Geography and Map Divisions, are essential for the study of Central America in the mid-nineteenth century. Squier (1821–1888), author of *Ancient Monuments of the Mississippi Valley* (1848), *Nicaragua* (1852), *Notes on Central America* (1855), *Honduras* (1870), and *Peru* (1877) and a U.S. diplomat and entrepreneur, had maintained an impressive collection of papers on his anthropological research and diplomatic and business activities in Central America and Peru, including correspondence, business records, manuscripts for publications, and related materials from 1841 to 1888. A group of thirty-eight maps of Central America and Peru drawn or annotated by Squier provides detailed information on Honduras, El Salvador, and Nicaragua. These materials, compiled primarily for Squier's nineteenth-century canal and railway initiatives in Central America, provide a glimpse into the intense U.S.-British rivalry in Central America when Squier was diplomatic representative.

The Manuscript Division also has the papers of Central American filibusters William Walker and David Deaderick and the Guatemalan documents collection which contains some 35,000 items pertaining to government agencies, political parties, and labor unions (1944–1954) during the Arévalo and Arbenz presidencies. The papers of Chandler P. Anderson, in the Manuscript Division, relate to the international diplomatic and arbitration efforts of a lawyer in Central America, Cuba, and Panama, including records on the Hay-Paunceforte Treaty, the Chamizal (Mexico) case, the Nicaragua-Honduras boundary dispute (1920–1921), Nicaraguan politics, and Panama-Costa Rica boundary disputes (1914–1932).

Le Chimborazo vu depuis le Plateau de Tapia. In Alexander von Humboldt and Aimé Bonpland. Voyage de Humboldt et Bonpland . . . Ière partie; relation historique . . . Paris, F. Schoell, 1810. Snow-capped peaks, high arid plateaus, and deep luxuriant valleys all character- ize one of the natural land formations most often associated with South Amer- ica: the mountain system known as the *Cordillera de los Andes.* From 1799 to 1804, the renowned explorer and naturalist Alexander von Humboldt, accompanied by the botanist Aimé Bonpland, made a scientific excursion to South and Central America collecting numerous plant spec- imens and studying flora, fauna, and ge- ology. Chimborazo, a formidable extinct volcano of some 22,000 feet, is situated in central Ecuador. In pre-Conquest times, it was located in the northern part of the Inca empire. For a long pe- riod, it was considered the highest An- dean mountain. *(Rare Book and Special Collections Division)*

Négresses allant a l'Eglise pour être baptisées. Engraving. By Jean-Baptiste Debret. Voyage pittoresque et historique au Brésil, Vol. 3. Paris 1834–39. (Rare Book and Special Collections Division)

International interest in the construction of an interoceanic canal across the Central American isthmus is extremely well documented in the Library of Congress. The JOSEPH AND ELIZABETH ROBINS PENNELL COLLECTION, in the Prints and Photographs Division, contains copies of Joseph Pennell's graphic prints on the construction of the Panama Canal. In 1978 the Library acquired the PANAMA CANAL ZONE LIBRARY—MUSEUM COLLECTION which documented the U.S. role in the Panama Canal Zone in the twentieth century. This multiformatted collection has been disbursed throughout the Library, with rich holdings in the Geography and Map and Serial and Government Publications Divisions, as well as the general books collection. The papers of George W. Goethals and William Gorgas on Panama Canal construction are in the Manuscript Division, as are those of Philippe Jean Buneau-Varilla which address French and United States efforts to build a canal in Panama by one of its participants, the Nicaraguan Canal Construction Company (1886–1891) and of Lewis Haupt (Nicaraguan Canal Project 1861–1923) and of the numerous surveys by U.S. representatives,

including those of naval officer Charles Whiteside Rae of the Isthmus of Tehuantepec (1870–1871), naval officer Thomas Oliver Selfridge, Jr.'s correspondence and maps relating to his survey of the Isthmus of Darien for a proposed interoceanic canal (1869–1874), and naval officer Robert Wilson Shufeldt's correspondence and maps pertaining to his 1870 to 1871 survey expedition in Tehuantepec in search of a trans-Isthmus canal route.

The Library's materials on modern Mexico are particularly extensive. The Manuscript Division has a collection of manuscripts, military diaries, correspondence, family documents of Mexican Emperor Agustín de Iturbide (1799–1876), and correspondence of Mexican President Antonio López de Santa Anna. The Microform Reading Room has, on seventy-two reels of microfilm from the Banco de México, the papers of Matías Romero, Mexico's diplomat in the United States from 1864 to 1867. The ARCHIV KAISER MAXIMILIANS VON MEXIKO COLLECTION, in the Manuscript Division, contains photocopies of Austrian archival documents pertaining to the French occupation of Mexico, 1861–1865, and the Microform

Reading Room has the ARCHIVO MAXIMILIANO DE HAPSBURGO (a seventy-four-reel microfilm collection from Mexico's *Instituto Nacional de Antropología e Historia* (INAH) which contains copies of manuscripts and printed materials from the nineteenth century on the reign of Maximilian in Mexico including letters, telegrams, circulars, decrees, broadsides, poems, newspaper and magazine articles, and speeches, covering political and military affairs, international relations and diplomacy, and legal, commercial, and financial matters.

The impact of the early twentieth-century revolution in Mexico is documented by substantial materials in the Library of Congress. The Manuscript Division has army officer John L. Hines's annotated photoprocessed intelligence maps showing the operations of General John J. Pershing's 1916 Punitive Expedition in Mexico as well as Pershing's papers. The Microform Reading Room has the papers of Adalberto Tejeda (governor of the state of Vera Cruz, 1920–1924); the ARCHIVO DE DON FRANCISCO I. MADERO (on twenty-two reels of microfilm from the collections of Mexico's INAH), containing handwritten, typed, and printed materials from the late nineteenth and early twentieth centuries dealing with that Mexican president's public life and in which are found letters, telegrams, circulars, bills, newspaper and magazine clippings, business orders and accounts, the handwritten original of Madero's classic work, *La sucesión presidencial*, and coverage of Madero's presidential campaign in Mexico in 1910 and other political matters; and the ARCHIVO DE LA REVOLUCION MEXICANA (on eighty-five reels of microfilm from Mexico's INAH), which is a collection of bound typewritten transcripts of diverse printed and manuscript originals from the seventeenth through the twentieth centuries dealing with the issues, institutions, and personalities of the Mexican Revolution.

The Library's collection of materials on nineteenth- and twentieth-century Cuba is quite rich. Among these materials are found, in the Manuscript Division, the Juan and Nicolás Arnao papers (1868–1898), of these two Cuban revolutionaries among whose papers are found revolutionary publications and letters from José Martí, Máximo Gómez, and Antonio Maceo; the Domingo del Monte collection of manuscripts pertaining to Cuban history (1500–1869) with substantial holdings on colonial administration, military affairs, and nineteenth-century abolitionist and revolutionary activities; and the papers of José Ignacio Rodríguez (1860–1907), a Cuban in the United States, who served in the Bureau of American Republics and as the first librarian of the Columbus Memorial Library, and later of the Organization of American States. His collection also includes the papers of the Cuban reformer José Manuel Mestre and of Cuban

NUMERO 1.
CALAVERAS DEL MONTON.

Es la vida pasajera
Y todos pelan el diente,
Aquí está la calavera,
Del que ha sido presidente.
También la de Don Ramón
Y todos sus subalternos
Son como buenos Gobiernos
Calaveras del montón.

No caven ya en el Panteón
Es mucha la guesamenta,
Entre ellas también se cuenta;
La de Landa y Escandón.
Que les prendan sus siriales
A nombre de la Nación
Alcabo que son iguales;
Calaveras del montón.

Las otras son de Oficiales
Sin ninguna distinción,
Coroneles. . . . . Generales
Y jefes de división.
Mayores con charreteras
Capitanes de instrucción,
Toditos son calaveras
Calaveras del montón.

A la vez los ayudantes
Con todito su Escuadrón.
Y siguen los Aspirantes:
Calaveras todos son.
Calavera es el Teniente
Y también la reclusión,
Y lo mismo el subteniente
Calaveras del montón.

Esto si que es un recreo
Nadie de morir se escapa
A las muertes con su capa
Diciendo misa las veo;
Y responsos para el Papa.
Ya le prendieron sus ceras
Y se hayan en oración
Calaveras del montón.

También al fuereño toca
Su partesita en la fiesta,
Que por abrir la boca;
Un eléctrico lo acuesta.
Estas si que son tonteras
El andar en la función,
Toditos son calaveras
Calaveras del montón.

Muchos hicieron corajes
Y sucumbieron de enojo,
Fueron grandes personajes:
É hicieron todo á su antojo.
Como fieles y constantes
De su patria en la Nación;
A hoy los representantes
Calaveras todos son.

Empesamos por el chino
Y vamos viendo despues,
Que al llegar á su destino;
Murió con el Japones.
La china fué la primera
Un representante envió,
Y se quedó calavera;
De tantas cosas que vió.

España un enviado dió
Que fué especial y muy fiel,
Pues al momento cumplió,
Con el encargo del Rey.
Tu persona placentera
Va en mi representación,
Pero quedó calavera
Calavera del montón.

Los valientes tiradores,
Soldados de artillería
Juntos con los zapadores;
Calaveras son en este día
El soldado de primera
Y el cabo de pelotón;
Con su horrible calavera
Espantan en el panteón.

Calaveras por millares
Se van contando por cientos,
Todos fueron militares;
Y pasaron por sargentos
Comandantes de sección
Que se numere la hilera
Que grite la calavera:
Ya estamos en el panteón.

Ya se llenó el panteón
No queda ni un ahujero,
Pues se cuentan por montón;
Calaveras por entero.
Hoy el sepulturero
Escarba como una fiera,
Y busca la calavera;
De Don Francisco Madero.

Que de pezar se murió
Sin encontrar á la suerte;
La muerte se lo llevó
En su lomo como fuerte.
Madero murió inosente
Pero quedó la madera
Por querer ser presidente
Lo volvieron calavera.

Todo charlatán pulquero
Que á mujeres engañó,
Calavera se volvió;
Tan solo por embustero.
Aquél que vendió su quezo
Con la muerte allá en la plaza,
Se ha quedado como tiezo
Calavera de su casa.

El vendedor de las peras
Los saca muelas chorriados,
Se han quedado calaveras;
Y con los dientes pelados.
Y aquellos que se murieron
Enfermos del corazón.
Ya sus velas les prendieron;
Calaveras del montón.

Ya las inditas placeras
No hicieron buena fortuna,
Por andar vendiendo tuna;
Se volvieron calaveras.
Lo mismo el del chicharrón
Y todas las enchiladeras;
Son roidas calaveras,
Calaveras del montón.

Imprenta de Antonio Vanegas Arroyo.—2a Calle de Santa Teresa, Número 43.—México año de 1910.

Carnival Havana 1952. Half tone and lithographed poster. 1952. Carnival originated in Europe in the Middle Ages to portend the start of Christian Lent and symbolically celebrate the death of winter and the beginning of spring. In the Luso-Hispanic world, it is observed annually throughout the Americas and the Iberian Peninsula, with noteworthy celebrations in Rio de Janeiro, Salvador (Bahia), Port of Spain, and New Orleans. *(Poster Collection, Prints and Photographs Division)*

South view of the town & fortification of
Puerto Rico [1874]

American political societies. The Recorded Sound Reference Center of the Motion Picture, Broadcasting, and Recorded Sound Division has an extensive collection of commercial and noncommercial recordings, including 230 radio monitorings of Fidel Castro's speeches.

The first independent Latin American nation, Haiti, is represented by extensive holdings, among which is found a collection of original addresses and proclamations for the period 1798–1800 of Haitian liberator Toussaint L'Ouverture, in the Manuscript Division, and a selection on microfilm of portions of the Mangones collection of books and manuscripts on independence and the early national period, in the Microform Reading Room.

The papers of various U.S. citizens involved in inter-American affairs, in the Manuscript Division, include those of Presidents Thomas Jefferson, James Madison, James Monroe, James K. Polk, U. S. Grant, William McKinley, Theodore Roosevelt, William Howard Taft, Woodrow Wilson, and Warren G. Harding; of U.S. Secretaries of State, such as Henry Clay, William Marcy, James G. Blaine, Richard Olney, John Hay, Philander C. Knox, Charles Evans Hughes, Cordell Hull, and Henry Kissinger; and of special diplomats Joel Poinsett, Jeremy Robinson, Nicholas B. Trist, John Barrett, and Josephus Daniels.

Involvement in the affairs of various Latin American nations are reflected in the papers in the Manuscript Division of P. G. T. Beauregard, Winfield Scott, David Connor (U.S.-Mexican War 1846–1848), George Dewey and Pascual

A view of the town and fortification of [San Juan] Puerto Rico [1824]. Original watercolor. San Juan, Puerto Rico's most populous municipio, its cabecera, which is the capital, was founded in 1521. It is the second oldest capital city in the hemisphere. During the sixteenth century, San Juan was a departure point for Spanish exploration and colonization, and its location was a strategic military site in the Caribbean. In 1647 Felipe IV called it the key and vanguard of all the West Indies. Among the major fortifications are El Morro Fort begun in 1539, the city wall, begun in the 1630s, and Fort San Cristóbal, built in 1765. By the midnineteenth century San Juan was totally fortified. (Prints and Photographs Division)

OPPOSITE TOP. *[Portion]. Croquis de la Ysla de Balanguingui y sus adyacentes en el Archipielago de Jolo [Philippines] . . . 1848. . . . J. Espejo. 1848.*

OPPOSITE BOTTOM. *[Panoramic view of Fort Sipac].* Spain maintained administrative and military control of the Philippines from Magellan (1521) until the Spanish American War (1898). This map was prepared following the expedition directed by the governor Narciso Clavería against rebellious moros of Balanguingui who had taken more than 200 captives during the revolt. This map from the collection of the Real Escuela de Navegación de Cádiz is part of a unique collection of nearly 400 manuscript maps and charts of various parts of the Hispanic world acquired by the Library of Congress from Maggs Brothers, London in the 1920s. *(Maggs Map Collection, Geography and Map Division)*

Cervera (Spanish American War), Leonard Wood (U.S. Army of occupation in Cuba), and in the papers of private citizens and organizations including those of Mary Mann (correspondent on educational initiatives with Sarmiento, Mitre, and other nineteenth-century Argentine leaders), Clara Barton (Spanish American War), and the Women's Auxiliary Conferences of Pan American Congresses (minutes and correspondence, 1915–1927). The Geography and Map Division possesses an original manuscript map of the U.S. siege of Vera Cruz during the U.S.-Mexican War, prepared by P. G. T. Beauregard, and photocopies of Robert E. Lee's map collection from that same war.

Discussions of inter-American commercial interests are found in the papers of Riggs and Company (Central and South America, 1816–1854) and the National Citizens Committee on Relations with Latin America (financial and banking matters, 1905–1921), in the Manuscript Division, and the 214-reel microfilm collection, the GIBBS ARCHIVE: THE PAPERS OF ANTONY GIBBS & SONS, 1744–1953, in the Microform Reading Room, which consists of the family papers, and the business archives of Antony Gibbs and Sons, 1808–1969, a British business firm with particularly strong interests in Spain, Peru, Chile, Bolivia, and Brazil.

The Manuscript Division's collection of the papers of U.S. Latin American specialists include those of James A. Robertson, Samuel Guy Inman, and Howard F. Cline, a former chief of the Library's Hispanic Division.

The first printed maps of independent Venezuela, Colombia, Peru, Mexico, Argentina, Brazil, and Chile are located in the Geography and Map Division. In that collection the researcher can find items ranging from general maps for every country and period to detailed plans from the 1920s of Cuban sugar warehouses among its fire insurance maps. There are literally tens of thousands of maps for Latin America in the collection, including those in the Nicaraguan Canal Construction Company papers (with field survey books and soundings, 1887–1913), to the most recent cartographic data for each country. More than 960 separate map series, on topics such as topography, hydrography, geology, city planning, and soil types for various countries of Latin America and the Caribbean are available. Large quantities of nautical and hydrographic charts produced by Argentine, Brazilian, and Chilean governmental agencies are supplemented by comprehensive holdings of U.S. Coast and Geodetic Survey, British Admiralty, French Hydrographic Office, Spanish and Portuguese Marine, and U.S. Hydrographic Office charts.

Additional items of interest in the study of nineteenth- and twentieth-century activities in Latin America and the Caribbean are located in the Manuscript Division. Among these items are notebooks compiled by John Bull during the

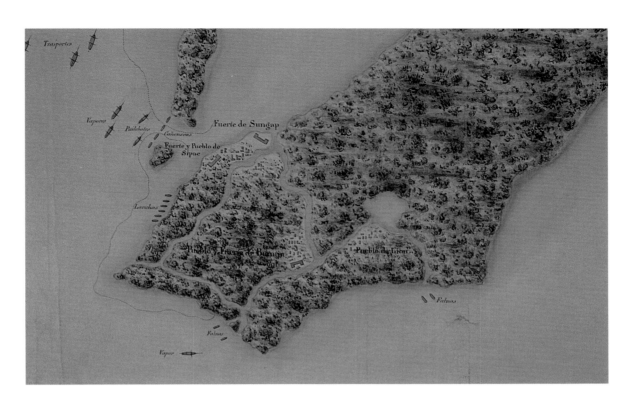

Trasportes

Vapores

Pailebotes

Cañoneras

Fuerte de Sungap

Fuerte y Pueblo de
Sipac

Lanchas

Pueblo y Fuerte de Bunug

Pueblo de Liun

Faluas

Faluas

Vapor

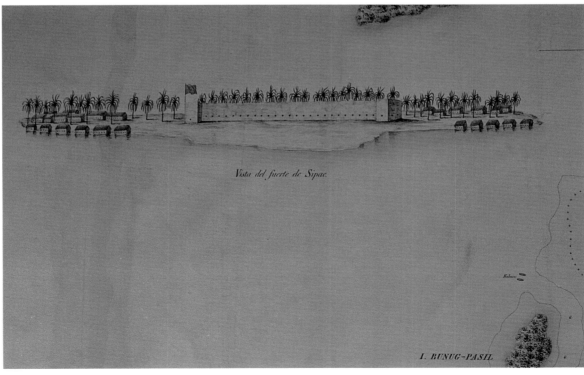

Vista del fuerte de Sipac.

Faluas

I. BUNUG-PASIL

Street scene. Bogotá, Colombia. [1940]. Bogotá was founded as Santa Fé de Bogotá in 1530 by Gonzalo Jiménez de Quesada. Charles V gave the city a coat of arms and made it the seat of the audiencia of New Granada in 1548. It became the capital of the Viceroyalty of New Granada in 1717 and the capital of independent Gran Colombia in 1821. Today, it is the capital of Colombia. In 1948, it served as host to the Ninth International Conference of American States at which the draft charter of the Organization of American States and the Pact of Bogotá, calling for peaceful settlement of disputes among American nations, were approved. *(Archive of Hispanic Culture, Prints and Photographs Division)*

U.S.-Mexican boundary commission survey of 1850; John Wills Greenslade's papers and aerial oblique photographic prints and manuscript maps of areas selected in 1940 for proposed naval air bases in Antigua, the Bahamas, Bermuda, British Guiana, Jamaica, Martinique, St. Lucia, and Trinidad; and Francis LeJau Parker's manuscript maps depicting the Tacna Arica boundary dispute between Chile and Peru.

The FARM SECURITY ADMINISTRATION COLLECTION, in the Prints and Photographs Division, is probably the most famous pictorial record of American life in the 1930s. Roy E. Stryker, formerly an economics instructor at Columbia University, began this documentary project in 1935 for the Farm Security Administration (FSA). Some of the photographers in the small staff were Jack Delano, Walker Evans, Dorothea Lange, Russell Lee, Carl Mydans, Arthur Rothstein, Ben Shahn, John Vachon, and Marion Post Wolcott. This collection is invaluable for its graphic representations of the impact of the Depression on portions of the Luso-Hispanic American community in the 1930s.

The staff initially photographed the lives of sharecroppers in the South and migratory agricultural workers in the Midwest and West. As the scope of the project expanded, the photographers documented rural conditions throughout the nation, life in urban communities, and the domestic impact of the war effort. Approximately 164,000 original FSA negatives, 2,600 Kodachrome transparencies, 75,000 photoprints, and some photographers' notebooks were transferred to the Library of Congress in 1944.

In the Motion Picture and Television Reading Room are found documentaries of living conditions and news events on Latin America, from 1890s scenes of Mexico, Porfirio Díaz, and the Spanish American War to film footage of Argentine President Juan Perón. There also exists a unique collection of rare footage of Theodore Roosevelt in Latin America, including his activities in the Spanish American War and later trips to Panama, the Amazon, and Colombia.

The PEABODY MUSEUM COLLECTION, a collection of sound recordings from the 1890s to the 1910s, in the Archive of Folk Song, is the result of the first documented use of mechanical recording equipment for ethnological research, by Jesse Walter Fewkes, an anthropologist affiliated with the Peabody Museum of Archaeology and Ethnology of Harvard University. Fewkes successfully recorded the speech and song of the Passamaquoddy Indians of Maine in March 1890 using a wax cylinder phonograph. He took the device on subsequent expeditions among the Zuñi and Hopi Indians of Arizona in 1890 and 1891. In 1970 the Peabody Museum presented to the Library a collection of early ethnological recordings which included over fifty of these historic Fewkes cylinders including a Mexican *pastores* collection dating from the turn of the century.

The Library of Congress has acquired through purchase or gift extensive holdings of major Latin American newspapers (now on microfilm) including *El Mercurio* (Valparaiso and Santiago, Chile), 1827 to date; *Jornal do Comercio* (Rio de Janeiro), 1827 to date; *El Siglo Diez y Nueve* (Mexico City), October 1841-June 1896; *O Estado de São Paulo* (Brazil), 1875 to date; *Excelsior* (Mexico City), 1918 to date; *El Comercio* (Lima), 1839 to date; *La Gaceta Mercantil* (Buenos Aires), 1823–1852; *La Nación* (Buenos Aires), 1891 to date; *El Día* (Montevideo), 1890 to date; *La Estrella de Panamá* (Panama City), 1858 to date; *Diario de la Marina* (La Habana), 1832–1959; and *El Tiempo* (Bogotá), 1911 to date. For the study of Luso-Hispanic American groups, the Library has consistently included among its collecting activities the acquisition of newspapers from throughout the community including copies of *La Prensa* (New York, 1940–1968); *Gráfico* (New York, 1916–); *La Opinión* (Los Angeles, 1926–); *The Brasilians* (New York, 1973–); and *Luso-Americano* (Newark, 1975–).

A collection of nineteenth- and early twentieth-century Mexican periodicals and newspapers, the HEMEROTECA HISTORICA MEXICANA COLLECTION from Mexico's *Instituto Nacional de Antropología e Historia*, is located in the Microform Reading Room. Such titles as *El Ateneo, El Ferro-Carril, La Aguila Mexicana, Diario del Gobierno de la República Mexicana, Mefistofeles, La Democracia: Periódico del Gobierno de Oaxaca, Revista Telegráfica de México, La Aurora Literaria, Correo Semanario de México, La Escuela Nacional de Artes y Oficios,* and *El Telégrafo Americano* are found there.

The legal materials of Latin American and Caribbean nations—the laws of nations, legislation, and official gazettes—are the strongest collection of any institution in the world. As one follows the progression of legal histories of the Americas, the complete sets of the congressional debates of national congresses, in the general books collection and on microfilm in the Microform Reading Room, are primary sources for the study of government in creation. A nearly one thousand-microfiche record of the *Historia de los debates legislativos en México*, from 1821 to 1991, is found in the Microform Reading Room.

Also available on microform are the official publications of the Organization of American States, the United Nations, the League of Nations, and the Foreign Broadcast Information Service and an estimated 98 percent of all U.S. doctoral dissertations that appear in *Dissertation Abstracts*.

Contemporary political issues in Latin America have not escaped the Library of Congress's collecting interests. The Microform Reading Room has the *Colección de documentos para la historia de la oposición política al estado autoritario en Chile 1973-l981*

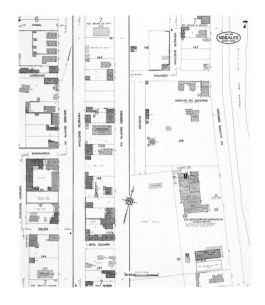

Fire Insurance Map of Nogales, Mexico 1931 (sheet 7). Pelham, N.Y.: Sanborn Map Company, 1931. A city in the state of Sonora, Mexico, Nogales was formed as a railroad town in the late nineteenth century and served as a gateway between the United States and Mexico. The fire insurance map of a portion of the city provides detailed information on businesses, building construction, and other features. The Kuomintang Chinese Society headquarters is located in the central portion of the map. Several other Mexican communities and various industries in Cuba are represented in the Sanborn map series. These maps are particularly useful to those involved in urban and social history as well as urban design. *(Geography and Map Division)*

Black musicians, a female dancer and costumed figure under a moon. Miguel Covarrubias. 1920. Covarrubias 257 A size. Miguel Covarrubias (1904–1957) was a Mexican writer, artist, ethnologist, and archaeologist. At the age of sixteen he taught art in the national education project initiated by Minister of Education José Vasconcelos. In the 1920s he went to New York City where he gained commissions with *Vanity Fair* and the *New Yorker*, contributed a book of caricatures, and produced a work on peoples in Harlem, *Negro Drawings* (1927), of which the above view is a part. In 1939 Covarrubias painted six widely disseminated illustrated maps of the Pacific Basin for the Golden Gate Exposition in San Francisco. He returned to Mexico in 1940 to rediscover his homeland in the work *Mexico South* and his classic studies of Olmec art, *The Eagle, the Jaguar, and the Serpent* (1954) and *Indian Art of Mexico and Central America* (1957) which he both wrote and illustrated. Covarrubias's outstanding original collection is found in the Library's Prints and Photographs Division. Rare imprints of his materials are also located in the Rare Book and Special Collections Division. *(Prints and Photographs Division)*

(in four microfiches) which contains documents produced by central committees, political commissions, congresses, and other organizations of political parties in opposition to Pinochet in Chile including those of the Socialists, Christian Democrats, Radicals, and the Communists; *MAPU, Movimiento Acción Popular Unitaría, Chile* which is a nineteen-microfiche collection by *Información Documental de America Latina* on that Chilean party's activities from 1969 to the early 1970s; and *Partido Comunista de Chile*, which is a ninety-four-microfiche collection on the activities of the Communist Party of Chile from 1950 through 1973 and includes the official papers and complete holdings of *Principios* (the official journal of the party's central committee).

The Library's office in Rio de Janeiro acquired in 1987 *Pesquisa nunca mais*, one of a limited edition of twenty-five copies detailing human rights abuses in Brazil during the 1960s and the 1970s. The Hispanic Division's Reading Room maintains a large file of declassified documents on the conflict in El Salvador in the 1980s and early 1990s from various U.S. agencies.

A collection of over 11,000 items issued by sociopolitical, religious, labor, and minority grass roots organizations in Brazil between 1966 and 1992 was compiled by the Library of Congress's Overseas Operations Field Office in Rio de Janeiro. The series, *Brazil's Popular Groups 1966–1992*, on 141 reels of microfilm, is located

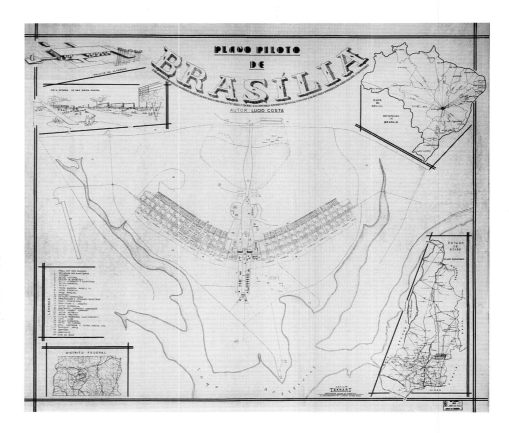

Plano piloto de Brasília. Lucio B. Costa. Abril 1958. The new capital of Brazil, in the state of Goiás, was designed and built under the direction of Lúcio Costa and Oscar Niemeyer. It was inaugurated on April 21, 1960. Brazilians from the eighteenth century had dreamed of relocating the national capital from the coast to the interior and wrote that dream into the 1891, 1934, and 1946 constitutions. President Juscelino Kubitschek announced his intention to relocate the capital and led the groundbreaking ceremonies on November 3, 1956. The city is planned on two axes, in the shape of a cross or a bird in flight, at right angles to one another. The east-west axis contains the political, administrative, economic, cultural, and recreational centers, and the north-south axis contains the residential districts. This map is the preliminary plan for the development of Brasília. *(General Collections, Geography and Map Division)*

in the Microform Reading Room. The microform collections *Iglesia en América Latina* and *Puebla 79* (by *Información Documental de America Latina*) are comprehensive compilations of documents relating to the activities of the Catholic Church in Latin America from CELAM II (1968) to CELAM III (1979).

The Library of Congress's holdings on Hispanic and Portuguese America, in which are found many irreplaceable treasures, have been assembled and supplemented for the advancement of the understanding of the Americas. The cult arose in Guatemala toward the end of the sixteenth century after a period of strife and turbulence between civil and ecclesiastical authorities. Although the adobe church was built relatively recently, its construction and decoration adhere to a pattern of missionary church building found elsewhere in New Mexico, which has its roots in the early church architecture of Mexico.

Retablo de Nuestro Señor de Esquipula, Chimayo, New Mexico [Altar Screen]. Watercolor. 1934. Little is known of the history of the church of the Santuario. It was commissioned by Bernardo Abeyta and was completed by 1816. Altar screens, like the one depicted, are especially ornate in their design and fabrication. This screen may have been painted by Molleno, sometimes knows as the Chili Painter, whose career spanned the period 1804 to 1845. The screen is conceived of as a stagelike space that focuses on the tabernacle frame; its complexity is best revealed in Spanish America where there was some fusion of indigenous expression with European elements. Nuestro Señor de Esquipula Church is associated with the cult of the Señor of Esquipula that emphasized Christ's healing and miraculous powers. The cult arose in Guatemala toward the end of the sixteenth century after a period of strife and turbulence between civil and ecclesiastical authorities. Although the adobe church was built relatively recently, its construction and decoration adhere to a pattern of missionary church building found elsewhere in New Mexico, which has its roots in the early church architecture of Mexico. *(Historic American Buildings Survey, Prints and Photographs Division)*

A Brief Researcher's Guide

The primary function of the Library of Congress is to serve the Congress. In addition, the Library provides service to government agencies, other libraries, scholars, and the general public. All researchers preparing to come to the Library are strongly encouraged to pursue preliminary exploration in public, academic, or special libraries, so that they can make efficient use of their time in the collections of the Library of Congress.

The Library of Congress is a research library whose collections are kept in restricted, closed stacks. The Library's lending is restricted to official borrowers. Under certain conditions, the Library lends materials from its collections to other libraries for the use of their readers.

THE HISPANIC DIVISION

The Library of Congress does not have separate Hispanic and Portuguese collections. Upon arrival at the Library of Congress, a researcher interested in the Luso-Hispanic world should consult with the reference specialists in the reading room of the Hispanic Division, located in the Hispanic Room on the second floor of the Thomas Jefferson Building (LJ 205). That room contains a specialized reference collection on Hispanic and Portuguese themes.

For materials other than periodicals or books from the general books collection, the researcher must visit one of the Library's specialized reading rooms. Generally these research areas have custody of material based on format rather than their geographic origin. So, graphic prints usually are found in the Prints and Photographs Division and maps are found in the Geography and Map Division. Occasionally, such items may appear elsewhere in the Library's collections. Maps and graphic prints in bound volumes can be found in the Rare Book and Special Collections Division. One of the essential tasks of the reference specialists in the Hispanic Division is to provide specialized assistance to a researcher seeking materials in this large and complex library of over one hundred million objects.

Each reading room offers finding aids, bibliographies, and pertinent reference materials as well as access to the Library's main computerized catalog. The Library's National Reference Service (NRS) provides information by telephone (202–707–5522). It directs reference calls or correspondence to the appropriate reading room as necessary.

The following is a list of the reading rooms and special collections, in addition to what is offered in the Hispanic Division, that could be of value for the researcher with an interest in the study of the Luso-Hispanic world:

AFRICAN AND MIDDLE EASTERN READING ROOM (Serving Hebraic and Near East Sections). Adams Building, LA 132

AMERICAN FOLKLIFE READING ROOM, Jefferson Building, LJ G17

OPPOSITE. *Fiestas de Verano y Carnaval 1938–39. Half tone and lithographer posted. 1938. Montevideo.* Carnival remains the annual high point of Uruguayan festivity. Occurring before Lent, the carnival season includes parades with flowered floats, and buildings are festooned with streamers and colored lights. Parades with marchers wearing garishly colored masks and costumes clog the streets. A major feature is the tablado, a lavishly decorated temporary stage, on which musicians, clowns, dancers, and mummers perform. From the poster it is evident that carnival falls at the end of the summer season in the southern hemisphere. *(Poster Collection, Prints and Photographs Division)*

BUSINESS REFERENCE SERVICES. Adams Building, LA 508

GEOGRAPHY AND MAP READING ROOM. Madison Building, LM B01

LAW LIBRARY READING ROOM. Madison Building, LM 201

LOCAL HISTORY AND GENEALOGY READING ROOM. Jefferson Building, LJ G20

MAIN READING ROOM. Jefferson Building, LJ 100

MANUSCRIPT READING ROOM. Madison Building, LM 101

MICROFORM READING ROOM. Jefferson Building, LJ 107

MOTION PICTURE AND TELEVISION READING ROOM. Madison Building, LM 336

NEWSPAPER AND CURRENT PERIODICAL READING ROOM. Madison Building, LM 133

PERFORMING ARTS READING ROOM. Madison Building, LM 113

PRINTS AND PHOTOGRAPHS READING ROOM. Madison Building, LM 339

RARE BOOK AND SPECIAL COLLECTIONS READING ROOM. Jefferson Building, LJ 256

RECORDED SOUND REFERENCE CENTER. Madison Building, LM 113

SCIENCE READING ROOM. Adams Building, LA 5010

Publications on the Hispanic and Portuguese Collections

The Archive of Folk Song in the Library of Congress. Washington: Library of Congress, 1977.

The Archive of Hispanic Literature on Tape: A Descriptive Guide. Compiled by Francisco Aguilera and edited by Georgette M. Dorn. Washington: Library of Congress, 1974.

Besso, Henry V. *Ladino Books in the Library of Congress: A Bibliography.* Washington: Library of Congress, 1963.

Brazil Recordings in the Archive of Folk Culture. Washington: Library of Congress, Archive of Folk Culture, 1990. *LC Folk Archive Finding Aid Series.*

A Catalog of Brazilian Acquisitions of the Library of Congress, 1964–1974. Compiled by William V. Jackson. Boston: G.K. Hall, 1977.

Catalog of Broadsides in the Rare Book Division. Boston: G.K. Hall, 1972.

The Collection of John Boyd Thacher in the Library of Congress. 3 vols. Washington: Library of Congress, 1915–31.

Cuban Acquisitions and Bibliography: Proceedings and Working Papers of an International Conference Held at the Library of Congress, April 13–15, 1970. Compiled by Earl J. Pariseau. Washington: Library of Congress, 1970.

The Dayton C. Miller Flute Collection: A Checklist of the Instruments. Washington: Library of Congress, 1961.

De Vorsey, Louis, Jr. *Keys to the Encounter: A Library of Congress Resource Guide for the Study of the Age of Discovery.* Washington: Library of Congress, 1992.

Dorn, Georgette M. "Hispanic Books in the Library of Congress: 1815–1965" in *Philosophy and Literature in Latin America: A Critical Assessment of the Current Situation.* Albany: SUNY Press, 1989.

Federico García Lorca: A Bibliography. Compiled by Everette E. Larson. Washington: Library of Congress, 1987. *Hispanic Focus, no. 6.*

1492: An Ongoing Voyage. Edited by John R. Hébert. Washington: Library of Congress, 1992.

Green, Shirley L. *Pictorial Resources in the Washington, D.C. Area.* Washington: Library of Congress, 1976.

Grow, Michael. *Scholars' Guide to Washington, D.C. for Latin American and Caribbean Studies.* 2d edition. Washington: Smithsonian Institution Press, 1992.

A Guide to the Art of Latin America. Edited by Robert C. Smith and Elizabeth Wilder. Washington: U.S. Government Printing Office, 1948.

A Guide to the Collections of Recorded Folk Music and Folklore in the Library of Congress. Washington: Library of Congress, 1976.

OPPOSITE. *William Berryman. Jamaica Scene. Watercolor over grey ink and pencil on wove paper, ca. 1808.* English artist William Berryman, who spent eight years in Jamaica at the beginning of the nineteenth century, produced more than three hundred pencil and watercolor works of the island's people, landscape, housing types, and vegetation. *(Prints and Photographs Division)*

The Handbook of Latin American Studies. Vol. 1 (1936)—. Compiled in the Hispanic Division, Library of Congress. Edited by Dolores M. Martin. Austin: University of Texas Press.

Hanke, Lewis U. "The Luís Dobles Segreda Collection," *Quarterly Journal of the Library of Congress*, v. 1 (January/March 1944), 57–62.

Hans P. Kraus Collection of Hispanic American Manuscripts: A Guide, by J. Benedict Warren. Washington: Library of Congress, 1974.

The Harkness Collection in the Library of Congress: Calendar of Spanish Manuscripts Concerning Peru, 1531–1651. Washington: U.S. Government Printing Office, 1932.

The Harkness Collection in the Library of Congress: Documents from Early Peru, the Pizarros and the Almagros, 1531–1578. Washington: U.S. Government Printing Office, 1936.

The Harkness Collection in the Library of Congress: Manuscripts Concerning Mexico, A Guide. Washington: Library of Congress, 1974.

Hébert, John R. "Maps by Ephraim George Squier: Journalist, Scholar, Diplomat," *Quarterly Journal of the Library of Congress*, v. 29 (January 1972), 14–31.

The Hispanic Room in the Library of Congress. Hispanic Division, Library of Congress.

The Hispanic World 1492–1898: A Guide to Photoreproduced Manuscripts from Spain in the collections of the United States, Guam, and Puerto Rico/El mundo hispánico 1492–1898; guía de copias fotográficas de manuscritos españoles en los Estados Unidos de América, Guam y Puerto Rico. Compiled by Guadalupe Jiménez Codinach. Washington: Library of Congress, 1994.

Index to Latin American Legislation, 1950–1960. Compiled in the Hispanic Law Division. Boston: G.K. Hall, 1961. With supplements for 1961–65, 1966–70, 1971–75.

Kraus, Hans Peter. *Sir Francis Drake: A Pictorial biography.* With an historical introduction by David W. Waters and Richard Boulind and a detailed catalog of the author's collection. Amsterdam: N. Israel, 1970.

Latin America in Basic Historical Collections: A Working Guide. Compiled by Russell H. Bartley and Stuart L. Wagner. Stanford: Hoover Institution Press, 1972.

Latin American and Caribbean Recordings in the Archive of Folk Culture. Washington: Library of Congress, Archive of Folk Culture, 1984.

Latin American Newspapers in United States Libraries: A Union List. Compiled by Steven M. Charno. Austin: University of Texas Press, 1968.

Latin American Serial Documents: A Holdings List. Compiled by Rosa Quintero Mesa. (1968–73).

The Lessing J. Rosenwald Collection: A Catalog of the Gifts of Lessing J. Rosenwald to the Library of Congress, 1943 to 1975. Washington: Library of Congress, 1977.

List of Geographical Atlases in the Library of Congress, With Bibliographical Notes. 8 volumes. Washington: Library of Congress, 1909–74.

Lowery, Woodbury. *The Lowery Collection: A Descriptive List of Maps of the Spanish Possessions Within the Present Limits of the United States, 1502–1820.* Washington: U.S. Government Printing Office, 1912.

Mexican-American Folksong and Music on Field Recordings in the Archive of Folk Culture. Washington: Library of Congress, Archive of Folk Culture, 1982.

Mexico Recordings in the Archive of Folk Culture. Washington: Library of Congress, Archive of Folk Culture, 1990. *LC Folk Archive Finding Aid Series.*

Microfilmed Papers of José Ortega y Gasset Open for Research in the Library of Congress. Compiled by Everette E. Larson. Washington: Library of Congress, 1982. *Hispanic Focus, no. 2.*

Miguel de Unamuno: A Bibliography. Compiled by Everette E. Larson. Washington: Library of Congress, 1986. *Hispanic Focus, no. 5.*

Nautical Charts on Vellum in the Library of Congress. Compiled by Walter Ristow and R. A. Skelton. Washington: Library of Congress, 1977.

Patterson, Jerry E. and William R. Stanton. "The Ephraim George Squier Manuscripts in the Library of Congress: A Checklist," *Papers of the Bibliographical Society of America*, v. 53 (1959), 309–326.

Peruvian Field Recordings in the Archive of Folk Culture. Washington: Library of Congress, Archive of Folk Culture, 1982.

The Portuguese Manuscripts Collection of the Library of Congress: A Guide. Compiled by Christopher C. Lund and Mary Ellis Kahler. Washington: Library of Congress, 1980.

Puerto Rico Recordings in the Archive of Folk Culture. Washington: Library of Congress, Archive of Folk Culture, 1993. *LC Folk Archive Finding Aid Series.*

Ramón María del Valle-Inclán: A Bibliography. Compiled by Everette E. Larson. Washington: Library of Congress, 1986. *Hispanic Focus, no. 4.*

The Rosenwald Collection: A Catalogue of Illustrated Books and Manuscripts, of Books from Celebrated Presses, and of Bindings and Maps, 1150–1950, the Gift of Lessing J. Rosenwald to the Library of Congress. Washington: Library of Congress, 1954.

Selected Articles in the Library of Congress on Manuel Antonio Noriega. Compiled by Everette E. Larson. Washington: Hispanic Division, Library of Congress, 1990.

A Selective Listing of Monographs and Government Documents on the Falkland/Malvinas Islands in the Library of Congress. Compiled by Everette E. Larson. Washington: Library of Congress, 1982. *Hispanic Focus, no. 1.*

Sendero Luminoso: A Bibliography. Compiled by Everette E. Larson. Washington: Library of Congress, 1985. *Hispanic Focus, no. 3.*

Smith, Robert C. "The Archive of Hispanic Culture," *Quarterly Journal of the Library of Congress*, v. 1 (October/December 1943): 53–57.

A Survey of Cuban Revistas, 1902–1958. Compiled by Roberto Esquenazi-Mayo. Washington: Library of Congress, 1993.

Trinidad Field Recordings in the Archive of Folk Culture. Washington: Library of Congress, Archive of Folk Culture, 1982.

Winsor, Justin. *The Kohl Collection (Now in the Library of Congress) of Maps Relating to America.* Washington: Government Printing Office, 1904.

Works by Miguel de Cervantes Saavedra in the Library of Congress. Compiled by Reynaldo Aguirre. Edited by Georgette M. Dorn. Washington: Library of Congress, 1994.